S. Anthony of Padua

In Search of the

Evangelical Doctor

– PAUL SEVERN –

GW00503382

FASTPRINT PUBLISHING
PETERBOROUGH, ENGLAND

www.fast-print.net/store.php

S. ANTHONY OF PADUA IN SEARCH OF THE EVANGELICAL DOCTOR

Copyright © Paul Severn 2011

ISBN 978-184426-929-7

First published 2011 by
FASTPRINT PUBLISHING
Peterborough, England.

An environmentally friendly book printed and bound in England by www.printondemand-worldwide.com

Mixed Sources
Product group from well-managed forests, and other controlled sources
www.fsc.org Cert no. TT-COC-002641
© 1996 Forest Stewardship Council

PEFC Certified
This product is from sustainably managed forests and controlled sources
www.pefc.org
PEFC/16-33-415

This book is made entirely of chain-of-custody materials

Contents

Introduction

Many books have been written about S. Anthony of Padua over the years and it may well be wondered what more there is to be said. However, it seems to me that an examination of these books (at least those written in English) reveals that most books, although not all, concentrate on S. Anthony's life; his humility, his travelling and his preaching prowess. They tell of the marvellous miracles he performed and the wonders surrounding his death, and they tell of popular prayers and practices, novenas and litanies, and the devotions of the nine and thirteen Tuesdays.

All this is well and good, but it seems that the intellectual side of S. Anthony's life whilst acknowledged is left largely unexplored. Given that S. Anthony is a Doctor of the church, one of only thirty-something in two thousand years of church history and so declared on account of his eminent sanctity and profound learning (c.f. Huber p1) it seems to me that this is a striking omission. In this work then, I do not seek to correct or challenge what has gone before, nor will I dwell on the details of the saint's biography, but I wish to examine S. Anthony of Padua as a medieval intellect, a great scholar and a Doctor of the Universal Church. Having said this I am not motivated to write a complete and exhaustive intellectual history, but rather to offer a concise and accessible overview to act as a balance, to complement and augment the many available biographical works.

To put this in another way, I wish to redress what I perceive as an imbalance, and I am motivated by the question: exactly why was S. Anthony of Padua declared a doctor of the church? At one level we have a ready answer. Pope Benedict XIV (1740 – 1758) taught that three things are required for a saint of God to be honoured as a Doctor of the Church: firstly eminent sanctity, secondly profound learning and thirdly the official designation of the church. S. Anthony's eminent sanctity does not seem in question and the designation of the church is not one which I wish to dispute. That leaves S. Anthony's profound learning.

Before we embark on an exploration of S. Anthony's profound learning we might pause to consider what profound learning consists of. What are we looking for or what does profound learning (in the context) mean? It seems to me that there are three main things. Firstly the ideas of even the most original thinkers do not spring unbidden from nowhere. They are prompted and nurtured by experience and reflection; they are developments of what has gone before. Hence, we must examine those ideas, doctrines and ways of living that influenced S. Anthony most. Secondly profound learning will be recognised by its fruits, and we must look in S. Anthony's own writings for originality, both in terms of new thoughts and new ways of expressing what has gone before. Thirdly, profound learning is likely to have considerable influence, both in its own day and in generations to come and we must search for signs of S. Anthony's originality and influence in subsequent intellectual history. Therefore to summarise, a full answer to our question must examine the influences upon S. Anthony, S. Anthony's own work and the influence that his work had on his cultural, intellectual and spiritual successors.

This is the task I set myself, first and foremost Anthony's upbringing, education and indeed formation as an Augustinian canon must be examined, for as an Augustinian the intellectual foundations of Anthony's life were laid. Secondly the influence of S. Francis and his followers must be considered, for it is this influence that changed Anthony's life and brought it to maturity. I shall consider these two influences in section one.

Having done this I consider Anthony's own thought and theology in the light of the above. The main source for this is the still extant Sermons for Sundays and Feast Days. These are not sermons in the modern sense, but *sermones*, guides, or outlines written by S. Anthony for his brother friars to help them in their preaching. I shall consider these and the main theological themes that emerge from them. I shall consider Anthony's biblical theology, and the Christology that emerges from it. I shall consider Mariology and Anthony's contribution to ecclesiology and his understanding of the religious life. Finally I shall consider Anthony as a mystic theologian. I shall discuss Anthony's theology both as designed to combat the heresies of the day and as original medieval thought. This will be section two.

Finally, in section three I shall consider the enduring influence of S. Anthony of Padua. I shall consider his canonisation as a saint and his proclamation as a Doctor of the Church. I shall consider Anthony as a biblical scholar in a post-scholastic age and I will consider parallels between Anthony's work and the Second Vatican Council. I will finally suggest that Anthony's enduring legacy is an example of a life devoted to work and prayer. To conclude I will consider Pope John Paul II's letter on the fiftieth declaration of S. Anthony as a Doctor of the Church and I will suggest grounds for his enduring intellectual importance and consideration in the contemporary Church.

Before proceeding it seems fitting to give the briefest outline of our saint's life, to locate him historically and geographically. I acknowledge that there is some dispute and uncertainty about the precise details of the saint's life; these are not directly pertinent to my task and I accept the traditional account of his life without reserve. S. Anthony was born in Lisbon and baptized Fernando at the end of the twelfth century and according to tradition on 15 August 1195. He was born of well to do parents and educated as a boy at the school attached to Lisbon Cathedral. At the age of sixteen he entered the Augustinian priory of São Vicente outside Lisbon's walls where he remained for one to two years before being transferred to the Augustinian house in Coimbra, the Portuguese mother house of the day.

After about seven years in Coimbra (i.e around 1220) S. Anthony was released from his order, and took the Franciscan habit and the new name Anthony. He departed almost immediately to preach to the Muslims in Morocco, but his health failed him and he was too unwell to do any preaching. After a brief time and no success as an itinerant preacher he boarded a boat to return to Portugal which was blown off course and ship-wrecked on Sicily. Here he was nursed back to health, before travelling north with his brother friars to the great meeting of Franciscans at Assisi, known as the Chapter of the Mats, in (May) 1221. It is eminently possible, although not documented that S. Anthony met S. Francis, even if only in passing, at this time.

After the chapter, S. Anthony went to Montepaulo to a small hermitage when he spent a year in prayer and reflection, celebrating Mass for a small group of lay Franciscan brothers. His intellectual capacities had not yet been recognised by the Order, but these were spectacularly revealed when he was unexpectedly called upon to preach at a joint Franciscan / Dominican ordination in Forli. His eloquence and learning astounded everybody and he was immediately sent to be a preacher.

At first he preached in Forli and at nearby Rimini, and then further afield in northern Italy and as far away as southern France. He was also notably called upon by Francis to teach the brothers theology (about 1223) and was professor of theology at Bologna University. Exhausted by his travels S. Anthony settled near Padua around 1228, where he continued to preach (a series of Lenten sermons) and to teach, but also to write – and it was in this period that Anthony revised and completed his work on the *Sermones* which was begun in France.

In the convent of the Poor Clares at Arcella on 13 June 1231, S. Anthony died. He was canonised on 30 May 1232 and although Pope Gregory IX is said to have intoned the antiphon *O Doctor Optime*, and Anthony was honoured with the cult of Doctor of the Church, it was not formally declared until 16 January 1946 by Pope Pius XII in the encyclical letter *Exulta Lusitania felix*. After S. Anthony's canonisation, a basilica was built in his honour, to which his remains were transferred in 1263.

Section One

Sketching the Background

1.1   Augustinian Foundations

A manuscript of 1222, originating in the Augustinian Priory of Santa Cruz in Coimbra states "Among the Canons Regular of Santa Cruz at that time was the Reverend Father Anthony - whose name was Fernando Martini – a very learned and pious man, much distinguished in letters and illustrious by the abundance of his merits" (Ling p21, Maloney p21). Now whilst the reliability of this detail may be questioned, all of the historical sources do agree on the basic facts; that S. Anthony was transferred from his priory at Lisbon to the priory of *Santa Cruz* in Coimbra around 1212. Further the *Assidua*, Anthony's earliest biography, asserts that he was studious and scholarly. "He always cultivated his innate talents with special eagerness and exercised his mind with meditation" (*Assidua* p21).

This is significant for two reasons. Firstly it tells us that Anthony was considered as a learned man, 'distinguished in letters' when he was an Augustinian Canon. Of course we may infer this from his later preaching and teaching but this tells us that even as a very young man he was academically able. Hence he would have been fully conversant with the theological literature and discussion of the day. In other words in looking to Augustine as a key influence on Anthony we can be confident that the themes we explore and describe are ones which Anthony would have known. In other words he was not a simpleton to whom it would be inappropriate to attribute a mastery of Augustinian theology.

Secondly we can be sure Anthony studied at Coimbra. This is significant too, since Coimbra was the capital of Portugal at the time. Not only was it the centre of political scheming, but the presence of King Alfonso and his pious wife Queen Urraca meant that the priory of Santa Cruz was particularly well endowed. Independent texts speak of an unusually well-stocked library containing Aristotle and the ancient philosophers, commentaries on Holy Scripture and the works of the Fathers, including of course S. Augustine (c.f. Robson p161). We can assume that Anthony would have read and studied many if not all of these texts, and the variety and number of quotations in his written sermons would support this. Legend has it that Anthony also had a prodigious memory and that not only did he study many of these texts, but that he knew them off by heart.

Furthermore, in addition to the library, and no doubt partly because of it, Santa Cruz Priory was considered as an intellectual centre. With endowments from the Portuguese court some of the canons were enabled to travel abroad to study and most notable at the time were Master John and Master Raymund both of whom had studied at the University of Paris (c.f. Rohr p13-14), and who would have been at the cutting edge of contemporary theology (and science too). There is no doubt that they would have influenced intellectual life at Santa Cruz, and we can infer that Anthony's studies were not a dry and solitary affair but that he was part of a vibrant and flourishing intellectual community, where discussion, debate and of course teaching and learning of the highest standard went on.

The teachings and writings of S. Augustine were central to the theology of the day and as an Augustinian Canon,

Anthony would have not only studied Augustine but would have "lived Augustine" too. The works of Augustine may well have been a part of liturgical celebrations, read at meal times and great familiarity with the Rule of S. Augustine, which was to be read out once a week (c.f. Rule 8.2), may be assumed. It may be noted that when Lanfranc asked S. Anselm about his philosophical and theological ideas (in Monologion), Anselm replied that he had asserted "nothing which could not be immediately defended from canonical dicta or the words of S. Augustine" (Southern p71), and we may well imagine that although Anthony did not write anything at the time (that has survived) he too would have seen himself firmly rooted in a tradition based on the Bible and S. Augustine. What then was that Augustinian tradition?

Our answer to this must necessarily be incomplete and partial for this is not a text about Augustine. We cannot here give a full exposition of Augustine, and indeed it may seem an impossible task to capture anything of the breadth and depth of Augustine's thought in one introductory chapter but we can and must attempt to give an outline, to delineate the main themes, always remembering that we consider Augustine in order to more fully understand S. Anthony. Therefore fine details, subtle theological debates and points of interpretation must be ignored. When we come to consider Anthony more closely, it will be more profitable to do so against an Augustinian backdrop, however partial, rather than against no backdrop at all.

For Augustine theology was primarily about the bible, a science of holy scripture as it were, and Cooper describes "Augustine's relentless knocking at the door of scripture" (Cooper p183) and the key to this door was interpretation. Augustine tells us in his *Confessions* that he thought that parts of the Bible, particularly the Old Testament, if read literally were plainly wrong, but if interpreted correctly were a source of divine knowledge and delight. "Especially after I had heard one or two places of the Old Testament resolved, and oftimes 'in a figure' which when I understood literally, I was slain spiritually. Very many places then of those books having been explained I now blamed my despair in believing that no answer could be given to such as hated and scoffed at the Law and the Prophets" (*Confessions* V 24).

Having said this however, the idea that holy scripture needed interpreting was not new. Two main schools of biblical interpretation existed in the early patristic era. The first at Alexandria was centred around Christians like Clement and Origen whose work centred on allegorical exegesis. The central aim was to show that the Old Testament was not just Hebrew scripture, but was a book for Christians too, and that, if properly understood was profoundly Christological. Whilst there was much to be said for this position, there were dangers too. The first was that the literal meaning of the scripture was ignored or denied, and the second was that it encouraged the notion that scripture held secret knowledge or gnosis.

The second school was based at the other great Christian centre: Antioch. To put it very simply, critical exegesis was championed here, in contrast to allegorical exegesis. Lucian of Samosata, and others including to some extent John Chrysostom, paid more attention to the literal meaning of scripture, and also proposed a more-than-literal understanding. That is to suggest that the Old Testament prophets through vision or intuition could see the future through their own circumstances. The Old Testament prophet can both describe current events and their future fulfilment. Here the focus is on the human author (albeit inspired by grace) rather than hidden meaning in signs and symbols.

Augustine, although he entertained Manichaeism and a form of gnosticism in his early life, came to theological maturity under the influence of S. Ambrose, bishop of Milan. Augustine was not a formal pupil of Ambrose, indeed it seems Ambrose had little time for Augustine, but Augustine was deeply influenced by Ambrose's preaching. Ambrose traced a line back to S. Paul's dictum that "the written letters kill but the spirit gives life" (II Cor. 3:6), and hence the need for a spiritual or allegorical understanding of scripture. One of Ambrose's favourite themes is that "beneath the opaque and rebarbative 'letter' of the Old Testament, this 'spirit', the hidden meaning, calls to our spirit to rise and fly away into another world" (Brown P. p85).

In other words Augustine found 'the answer' to his troubles about the meaning of Holy Scripture by embracing the Alexandrian exegetical position, recognising multiple meanings in a given text – an outer fleshly meaning and an inner spiritual meaning. This is not to suggest a multiplicity of meanings, one of which is no better than any other, as in some post-modern sense, but is based on the conviction that the text points to reality and that reality expresses itself through the text. "Thus in the Gospel he speaketh through the flesh; and this soundeth outwardly in the ears of men; that it might be believed and sought inwardly, and found in the eternal Verity; where the good and only Master teacheth all His disciples" (Confessions XI 10).

As time progressed Antiochene exegesis became less influential and indeed was regarded with some suspicion by the Council of Constantinople II in 533 (c.f. Brown R. p1155). Alexandrian exegesis from Hilary through Ambrose and to Augustine blossomed and was the dominant approach to biblical interpretation, accepting both the Old Testament and the New Testament as Christian books. As Augustine famously has it "The New Testament lies hidden in the Old; and the Old Testament is enlightened through the New" *[In vetere novum lateat,et in novo vetus pateat]*.

This then is the principal or dominant teaching about the interpretation of Holy Scripture which S. Anthony would have received, and indeed when we come to consider his written sermons we shall see that this the exegetical method that he employs. Having considered Anthony's inheritance from S. Augustine concerning an approach to the understanding of Scripture we shall now turn to consider some of the other dominant themes in Augustine that would have influenced S. Anthony.

It is important to understand Augustine as an apologist – his work is driven by countering misunderstanding and heresy. Many of the doctrines he expounds are not new or original but they are presented in an especially clear way. We might speculate what Augustine's theology would have looked like if he had started with a *tabula rasa,* but the fact is that Augustine's theology is a response, a reply to heresy, and this apologetic mode gives Augustine's work a focus and a clarity that is remarkable.

Perhaps because of his philosophical background Augustine is particularly concerned with the nature of God. For Augustine, God is pure being, pure essence. He simply is, or as Cooper expresses it, "God was not a being like other beings, only greater; God was BEING" (Cooper p126). Furthermore the being that God has or is, is being in all fullness and perfection, and it is from God's absolute being that all other being, all other existence derives.

Furthermore when we seek the attributes of God we discover his ineffability. Whatever we try to say of God it falls short of the mark, and it is easier to say what God is not, than what he is. For example Augustine says that there are three types of being or three natures: bodies mutable in time and space, souls incorporeal but mutable in time and God who is neither corporeal nor mutable. He does not have a body, he does not change.

Things that we can say of God are inevitably very general, or simple in the appropriate sense. But again deriving his philosophy from the ancients, we must understand, says

Augustine, that since God is pure essence, He has no accidental qualities. As Augustine puts it, whatever He has, He is. In other words God is not wise, He is wisdom. He 'possesses' wisdom so completely and so fully that we have to say, He is wisdom. Similarly we do not say that God is good or just, but that so fully does God have these attributes that God is goodness, God is justice etc. Furthermore, in the Divine nature these natures are not properly distinct, for we cannot conceive of absolute justice apart from absolute wisdom, and in turn absolute goodness. The Divine attributes are not attributes as such but are dimensions almost, or modes of the Divine essence.

Finally, Augustine considers time and space at some length and ponders the relationship of God to time and space. In particular he says that all time past, present and future are present to God as an instant. God encompasses all time so He knows the future, but this is just as He knows the present and the past. It is not God's knowing of the future that *causes* it to be as some have believed, and thus seen Divine foreknowledge as a denial of human free will. Humans are entirely free to choose as they will; it is just that God sees these future choices as present.

Augustine is in no way threatened or unsettled by God's knowledge and power, he sees Him as a loving and benevolent father. He exclaims "O God You are the Father of truth, the Father of wisdom, the Father of the true and supreme life, the Father of happiness, the Father of the good and the beautiful, the Father of unintelligible light, the Father of our awakening and our enlightenment" (Soliloquia I 1,2). In the light of such remarks, some have suggested that Augustine over-emphasises God as God the Father, that he dwells excessively on the paternity of God, but this is unfair, since Augustine also has a well-developed Christology and of course writes at length on the Trinity.

Augustine's Christology is apologetic par excellence and is designed to combat the many and varied heresies and misunderstandings of the day, the details of which we must leave to one side. Augustine asserts Jesus Christ as truly God and truly man. This is neither the Godhead indwelling (temporarily) in a human body, nor a human exalted to the status of the Godhead, but two distinct nature or substances in one person. Augustine sometimes speaks of a 'mixture' but this is not to suggest that one nature somehow penetrates the other, but that the two are in perfect harmony. The human does not cease to be human nor does the Divine cease to be Divine. Theologians talk of a hypostatic union of the two natures.

Care must be taken however, since although the unity of Jesus Christ is made up of two natures, we must beware of locutions such as God born of a woman, or the death of God upon the cross. Augustine formulates the so called communication of idioms, not a person who is half God and half man, but "entirely God and entirely man" (*Sermones* 293, 7). This, says the modern Franciscan theologian Thomas Weinandy, is the key to understanding and clarifying the incarnation. Speaking of the suffering of Jesus Christ in particular, we have to say that although Jesus is one complete person, one complete entity, he suffered as a man. He did not suffer as God. In the same way as when Jesus ate we have to say Jesus ate as a man, because God does not have a mouth, teeth and a stomach (c.f.Weinandy p205). Indeed Jesus does everything He does as a man, otherwise the incarnation would mean God acting in man, which "the incarnation will never permit" (ibid).

A further exploration of Augustine's Christology leads to his teaching on the nature of redemption and the action of Divine grace. In *The Confessions*, Augustine recounts movingly his childhood theft of pears from a neighbour's tree. Crucially, the theft was not motivated by need, or indeed for any positive reason but was wholly gratuitous.

Augustine was not in any way ignorant, he knew the theft to be wrong, and indeed was motivated by the wrongness of the act. He writes, "Especially in that theft which I loved for the theft's sake; and it too was nothing, and therefore the more miserable I, that loved it" (*Confessions* II 16). Crucially Augustine did not perform this theft alone, and there was a social dimension to the act. Augustine no doubt wanted to be "one of the lads" as we might say, and upon later reflection sees a social context to sin, a collective guilt which is in need of a redemptive act. "But when it is said 'Let's go, let's do it' we are ashamed not to be shameless" (ibid. 17).

Collectively then we are in need of redemption, and faith teaches that Christ is our redeemer. But how does this work? Augustine teaches that the principal function or task of the redeemer is to act as a mediator, between God and man. Firstly, God cannot be the redeemer himself; the redeemer as God could not be an intermediary between God and man since the Divine Redeemer would be equally removed from us as God is himself. Equally the redeemer may not be regarded solely as a man, because how could a sinful man approach, let alone bargain or negotiate with the Divinity? In order then for Christ to be the redeemer he must be both God and Man. Augustine writes "From what He has of Himself, He is the Son of God; from what He has of us He is the Son of Man" (Sermons 127). He is, and indeed must be, both man and God and Augustine is thought to be the first, to describe Christ as *Homo-Deus*.

Having established that the redeemer must be *Homo-Deus*, the question arises, how is His redemption brought about? Augustine teaches that redemption is brought about on Calvary. In his crucifixion, Jesus took our sins upon Himself, and thereby our guilt and inevitable punishment have been cancelled. Jesus is the ultimate and perfect sacrifice for sins, who was prefigured in the ancient sacrifices of the Old Testament. In this final sacrifice however, Jesus both offers the sacrifice (He is the priest) and He is the victim. The sacrifice is offered freely out of love and as man Jesus can offer it on behalf of all men, and as God, the sacrifice is pure and acceptable.

Augustine teaches, because Jesus is *Homo-Deus*, that the sacrifice is fully efficacious and universal in its saving effects. The sacrificial death of Jesus on the cross makes us (men) co-heirs of God with Him, and through the cross we come to be partakers in the divine life. Further, as all men sin, Christ's redemptive act is for everyone, and we are all invited to share in the banquet of the kingdom.

The principal effect or fruit of Christ redemptive act is the out-pouring of divine grace. Augustine's theory of grace is a development of Pauline teaching, found mainly in the epistle to the Romans. Augustine's theology however takes this teaching to a wholly new level and is perhaps his greatest theological triumph – indeed Augustinianism is, in some quarters, considered primarily to mean Augustine's teaching on grace. Having said this Augustine's theology of grace is perhaps the most misunderstood and hotly contested part of his opus, but we must leave the details here to one side remembering we examine Augustine as a backdrop to understanding S. Anthony.

As I mentioned earlier much of Augustine's theology is apologetic, that is teaching to correct misunderstanding and more seriously, heresy, and the teaching on grace is no exception and may be seen as a counter to the Pelagians and the Manicheans. Further, Augustine's teaching on grace may be seen as a solution to a particular problem. The problem is this: on the one hand there is a philosophical difficulty. If God is the creator and author of all things and indeed knows all things how can men be free. If God has Divine foreknowledge how can men act freely, particularly in the moral sphere? On the other hand there is a theological difficulty, if Christ's influence and grace are admitted: "without Me you can do nothing" (John 15:5), then the freedom and autonomy of the individual (defining human characteristics at creation) seem to be further undermined.

In turning to Augustine's teaching it is important to realise it was not all delivered at one instant of time, but that these questions were a pressing concern over several years, and scholars debate the different nuances of Augustine's teaching over time. We may consider the most mature version of Augustine's theology of grace written in response to certain questions of Simplicianus, Ambrose's successor as bishop of Milan.

As we have already seen, for Augustine sin is not only individual but has a corporate or social dimension too, and so all men sin. Augustine rejects Pelagius' view that there could be a sinless perfect man, who was sinless and perfect on account of the actions of his own will. But this is not to say all are damned, for the human was created perfect in the image of God, and that fundamental 'Divine signature' remains. Humans after the fall are perhaps best understood as 'damaged goods', or as Augustine has it sick men in need of a physician. To continue the analogy, grace is the working or the healing of the physician. This healing is available to everyone and there is no sickness that cannot be cured.

But how does this connect with the problem of free will outlined above? Firstly Augustine teaches that grace is not a reward for good acts, or something that is given to those who are good and denied to those who are bad; but rather, grace is a Divine and unmerited gift *which enables* the human to do good acts. He writes "We know that grace…is given to adults for each and every good act" (Epistles 144, 2 Portalié p193), and as result the Divine remains the author and source of all that is good. Having said this, the human endowed with free will may still choose whether or not to accept the Divine gift of grace, for one can choose to act evilly, and no grace is here required. In other words humans cannot freely choose to be virtuous or to do good entirely of their own accord, but they can choose whether or not to accept the gift of grace which in turn enables them to do good. "Efficacious grace works infallibly, but never by an irresistible impulse, for even under its influence the will remains master of itself" (Portalié p198).

Without going further into the details we may note that the choice of the human after the fall is not the same as the choice of Adam. Adam could choose whether to act rightly or wrongly of his own accord. The human after the fall may choose whether or not to accept the gift of grace. Further we should note that Augustine distinguishes two types of grace, the grace given to all, even strangers for the exercise of natural virtue and grace given as preparation for supernatural acts which comes with Christian faith. How grace actually operates in or on the human person, and the problems which Augustine's account generate are topics we shall leave to one side here.

A number of other theological topics treated by Augustine may be seen in some sense as corollaries of Augustine's theology of grace. As we have seen Augustine vigorously proclaims the culpability of all men against the teachings of the Palagians, since all are party to a communal or social form of sin. However he makes one exception, namely the Blessed Virgin Mary. Augustine says relatively little about Mary, presumably because there were no great heresies of the day about Mary that needed countering, and indeed Augustine's mariology is not 'free standing', but is a direct consequence of Christological considerations. In so far as it was God's plan to send Jesus as saviour of the world, it was also part of his plan that humanity – represented *par excellence* by Mary – should cooperate in that plan.

Because Mary is mother of the Lord, she is in a unique place of privilege, the principal satellite of Christ as von Balthazar would have it (c.f. von Balthazar p208ff) and an overabundance of grace is bestowed on her so that she remains free of all sin, and remained a virgin even in childbirth. It is a contested question as to whether Augustine actually affirmed the doctrine of the immaculate conception of Mary. He seems to hint at it strongly without explicating the doctrine. Crucially Mary is exempt from original sin, not by right, but as a fact, in virtue of her motherhood of Him who is exempt by right (c.f. Portalié p176).

Augustine does not fail to draw out the more mystical considerations of Mary's virgin motherhood. For he says as Mary is mother of Christ she is mother of all His members, and hence is mother to us all. From the cross, Jesus told John "Behold thy mother" (John 19:27) and so all men may look to Mary as their mother. As mother of Christ, Mary is mother of the church, mother of all the baptised, and as great dignity is conferred on the church by Christ, so great dignity is conferred by Christ upon Mary. Augustine writes "Christ therefore, in order to make the virginity of the church in the heart, preserved the virginity of Mary in the body" (Sermons 188, 3).

The other main consequence of Augustine's teaching on grace is his theology of the church – which is classically apologetic and which may be understood on two fronts. Firstly in his teaching *contra* the Donatists, Augustine counters the schismatic state of the church in Africa. Following the death of the first bishop of Carthage, a number of local bishops hastily ordained Caecilius as his successor without waiting for a larger delegation of African bishops to arrive. These bishops deprived of exercising their choice and sorely affronted, declared the ordination invalid, and ordained a rival, named Majorinus who was in turn succeeded by Donatus. Many African Christians recognised Donatus but the original group of Catholics who ordained Caecilius did not, and in particular did not recognise the acts and ordinations performed by Donatus since his own orders were flawed. In the end Emperor Constantine ruled the Donatists to be in error and they were returned to the

Catholic fold by force, that is to say Donatist churches were forcibly closed.

In the mean time however, Augustine, by now catholic bishop of Hippo, was to debate with the Donatists, and argued that it was Divine grace and not human purity or worthiness that validated the Church and her sacraments. He argued that God had divinely instituted the church as a single and universal entity to preserve the correct transmission of truth entrusted by Christ to the Apostles, and to be the mediatrix, leading souls to salvation. Salvation is the final end of the church and Augustine echoes Cyprian's famous phrase "outside the Church there is no salvation".

Furthermore the church was vivified by the Holy Spirit, in a way that schismatic entities were not, and so she was enabled to perform her task of saving souls through the threefold ministry of teaching, governing and sanctifying. This task entrusted to the bishops as descendents of the apostles required the valid ordination of bishops, who in turn were answerable to the Petrine authority of the pope. By and through this structure the validity of all orders and sacraments was maintained.

The second and better known aspect of Augustine's teaching on the church stems from his controversy with the pagans and is found in the *City of God* – a twenty-two chapter work which took Augustine fifteen years to write. Augustine takes on the pagans who had suggested that the fall of Rome – the empire generally and the city of Rome in particular – was due to the new religion, i.e. Christianity, and the neglect of the traditional Roman gods. By city, Augustine means a whole human way of living, society, culture, law etc. and he contrasts the earthly city with the city of God. The earthly city exists to promote human ideals and goods, and whilst many of these are good and worthwhile, they are nevertheless limited and finite, and there will be endless squabbles over them. Of necessity the rich and the powerful will oppress the poor and the weak.

By contrast the city of God is ordered towards an external goal which is unlimited. Christians are pilgrims in the here and now travelling through the earthly city, but are true citizens of the city of God. Augustine claimed that even in the church we cannot be sure that all her members are citizens of God, for the church is made up of wheat and tares (c.f. Matt 13:24 ff), or in Augustine's memorable phrase, the church is "a mixed bag" (*corpus permixtum*). He writes "I have categorised the human race into two sub-species: one consists in those who live according to human standards and the other of those who live according to God. We also refer to them in a mystical fashion as two cities, that is, two societies of human beings one of which is predestined to rule with God for eternity and the other to undergo eternal punishment with the devil" (*City of God* XV 1). We should note that predestination here is in the sense discussed above: sinners are predestined to hell only by their own refusal to accept the gift of divine grace.

Although I have mentioned the vibrant academic community at Coimbra of which S. Anthony was a part, and I have mentioned that there were masters of theology from the Parisian school present at Coimbra at the time, I have written as though S. Anthony received his Augustinian influence from books alone. Of course, this was not the whole story, for via Master John and Master Raymund, S. Anthony would have been in touch with the highly influential Parisian Victorine school of theology – founded by Hugh of S. Victor (1096-1141). This school had experts in philosophy, theology and was also a centre for a great mystical movement which found inspiration in Hugh's own mystical theology. Therefore even if S. Anthony was not directly involved in the theological and philosophical debates, they would not have passed him by completely and he would have been very much aware of the latest intellectual developments.

There is much more that could be said about Augustinian theology, and mediaeval developments of it, but as a backdrop to a picture, it is necessarily painted in broad brush strokes, and serves principally to contextualise the detail concerning S. Anthony which will be the foreground. S. Anthony however was not only a scholar, he lived as an Augustinian Canon and so to complete this background, I now want to consider the influence that S. Augustine's rule would have had on the way Anthony lived. As an Augustinian Canon there is almost an organic connection, or a deep unity of purpose between him and S. Augustine which should not be neglected.

Augustine himself set up his first community at Thagaste in 388, almost as an extension of his family, and later he set up a more formal community at Hippo, which grew and expanded. He wrote his rule around 397, for this community. The idea of writing a rule for a community was not new. Pachomius and Horsiesius wrote rules for emergent monastic communities in the second and third centuries. We have the rule of S. Basil, written sometime shortly before Augustine's rule and so for Augustine to write a rule is quite in keeping with his position as a founder and a bishop. In time, S. Augustine's Rule was adopted by a whole family of religious communities, including Augustinian Recollects, Servites, Assumptionists and Dominicans.

Two things are particularly striking about Augustine's Rule. The first is its brevity – it is barely a dozen pages and deals with general themes and principles rather than details and particulars, such as we find in the sixty-three chapters of the later Rule of S. Benedict. Augustine's rule is more of a summary, a concise résumé of conferences and discussions that would have been (and still are) integral to communal life. This is, in part, what allows it to be widely applied, and to be relevant in a wide variety of contexts.

The second thing that is very marked is the rule's emphasis on community. At the heart of Augustine's view, its inspiration in fact, is that the monks should live together as the first Christian community in Jerusalem, sharing their goods, praying together and celebrating the Mass (c.f. Acts 4:31-5).The rule is a rule of the heart, a rule about an interior attitude or orientation, within community. Augustine is emphatic that the common life does not entail uniformity or identity, but equality under the law, based on the recognition that all humans are individuals. Each is to have what he needs: love of each for each is the key here.

The Rule's section on service is again not primarily about individuals but emphasises that "everything you do is to be for the service of the community" (Rule 5:2). Love is not self-seeking but puts the good of the community above love of the self. The Rule emphasises that the brother must obey his superior, but on the other side of the coin the superior must provide appropriate clothing, food, drink and other provisions for each brother as he requires. Books were particularly important for Augustine and one of the important provisions was a well-stocked library, which in turn was to feed and nourish the intellectual health of the monks.

The central work of the community is prayer and Augustine exhorts the monks to: "Persevere faithfully, in prayer (Col 4:2) at the hours and times appointed" (Rule 2:1). Augustine is not specific about details in the way that Benedictine is but is emphatic about the centrality of prayer, based on singing psalms and hymns. Again we see that when the brothers pray the words on their lips should also be alive in the hearts (Rule 2:3). It is interesting what Augustine says about words: firstly he says that whilst prayer is more than words, it is with words that Our Lord has taught us these essential things and so we should be attentive to them. Furthermore as the words are to be alive in the brothers' hearts, their prayers are not an extra or an adjunct to their lives but are to be at the very core of their lives. Their prayer is an essential expression of who they are.

In addition to the emphasis that common prayer should be celebrated properly, is the rule that the place of prayer should be kept available, so that the brothers should be able to pray privately at other times if they wish. However there is no specific emphasis on individual asceticism. There are no instructions to the individual about spiritual practices, and indeed putting the individual above the community in some kind of spiritual athletics competition would be quite foreign to the spirit of the rule. The monks are on their way towards God together!

This theme of prayer located within community would then be at the heart of Anthony's world-view as a mature Augustinian. A spirituality based on a desire for spiritual beauty, a common pursuit of the highest and the best of human life to be found in the perfection of God himself. This is no servitude, Augustinian life under a rule is a life of freedom; following Paul, Augustine contrasts Roman slaves with slaves to sin. Roman citizens are contrasted with men living freely by grace, not lawless, but free to respond to God and His law, as instantiated in the rule. The rule is both compassionate and optimistic. It is an invitation to live wholly in the spirit of Christ and as a follower of this rule, we see S. Anthony as serious and yet with a light touch, compassionate and optimistic too, living freely in love as part of a community, journeying towards its heavenly home.

1.2   Franciscan Influences

S. Francis was born in 1182, and although he followed his father into the cloth trade, he was enlisted into the army at the age of around twenty. Having been injured and struck by illness he was convalescing in Spoleto when he had a dream inviting him 'to follow the Master rather than the man'. He returned to Assisi, he gave alms to leper and in his own words, 'left the world'. In 1205 he heard a voice from a crucifix inviting him to 'go and repair my church' and he embarked on a life of prayer and a conversion to poverty.

By 1208 Francis had understood his vocation and drawn a group of followers around him, and drafted a simple rule. In 1210 Pope Innocent III gave Francis' order verbal recognition, and in 1212 a second order was founded with S. Clare, and annual general chapters were held from 1217. Francis retired as minister general of the Order in 1220 to be succeeded by Brother Elias. A new rule was drawn up in the early 1220s which underwent several revisions before it was finally approved in 1223 by Honorius III, and confirmed by the Papal Bull *Solet Annuere* of November 23. In the last two years of his life Francis wrote his famous Canticle of the Sun, and just before his death in September 1226 he dictated his Testament exhorting his brothers to follow the rule in poverty, simplicity and holy obedience.

According to most sources, S. Anthony moved from Lisbon to Coimbra in 1211 or 1212. Some five years later the first Franciscans arrived in Coimbra and begged for alms at the Augustinians' door. Again according to tradition Anthony got to know them and was impressed by their poverty and singular devotion to Christ. In 1220 the bodies of the first Franciscan martyrs were returned to Portugal and moved by this event, Augustinian Canon Don Fernando forsook his cloister and his white habit and joined the Franciscans taking the name Anthony.

Anthony was deeply moved by the martyrs who had laid down even their lives for Christ and requested to be sent immediately to Morocco to preach to the Muslims. His mission was a disaster, and returning from Africa by ship with his health in tatters he was blown off course to Sicily, where he was nursed by brother Franciscans, before travelling north to the 1221 Franciscan Chapter in Assisi. After the chapter Anthony was sent to Montepaulo where he lived for about a year as a near-hermit, thinking, praying and (although he did not know it) preparing for his public ministry.

All these dates are important, as they show that when Anthony joined the Franciscan Order it was barely ten years old. Therefore Anthony could not have been in receipt of a well-formed Franciscan theology and spirituality at the time of his joining or even by the time of his retreat at Montepaulo. Further, communications were not what they are today, and the transmission of ideas was necessarily a slow and somewhat haphazard affair. With eight hundred years of hindsight we must be particularly careful not to attribute Franciscan influences to Anthony that he simply could not have had at the time.

It seems to me that we can confidently identify three rudimentary Franciscan influences upon Anthony, which clearly coloured his thinking, and enabled him to build theologically upon his Augustinian foundations. The first of these is a commitment to poverty, and indeed an endorsement of Francis' love of Lady Poverty.

Anthony was first struck by the humility and simplicity of the mendicant friars who came to his door, and it is suggested that he was prompted to draw a comparison between their following of the Gospel, and his own life in a comfortable and richly endowed priory. Once he had become a Franciscan he would again have experienced and reflected upon poverty regularly, in Sicily and of course in Assisi and at Montepaulo.

Secondly, I think we may be confident that Anthony would have been familiar with Francis' writings, his rudimentary rule, and the later rule of 1220 and its various revisions, finalised and approved by Honorius III in 1223. Additionally Anthony would probably have read Francis' Canticle of Brother Sun (1225), possibly some of his other writings which were not extensive and almost certainly S. Anthony would have read Francis' deathbed Testament. Therefore I believe we may also legitimately consider these writings to be authentic Franciscan influences on S. Anthony too.

Thirdly, in his demand to be sent to Morocco, Anthony clearly wished to wear the martyrs' crown, and the mediaeval notion of self-sacrifice for the sake of the Gospel is something we need to explore. What is not clear is to what extent Anthony was influenced by Francis and Franciscans and to what extent he was influenced by the Fathers and his own ("non-Franciscan") experiences. What is clear is that Francis himself did seek martyrdom, even if Anthony did not know it at the time, and the return of the five Franciscan protomartyrs to Coimbra profoundly influenced Anthony, and seems to have been the catalyst that prompted him to act on his theological instincts. It will then be convenient to consider the medieval idea of martyrdom as a Franciscan influence, even if Franciscan influences were only one of several influences upon S. Anthony. Let us consider these in turn.

When the first friars came begging at the priory door in Coimbra, it is said that Anthony befriended them and asked about their way of life and their founder. What might they have told him? As has already been mentioned Francis was the son of a cloth trader and initially went into his father's business. He was a virtuous and generous man who had a concern for the poor and gave alms. One day working in his father's shop he failed to notice and ignored a beggar who entered the shop, so busy and distracted was he. Later he reproached himself and went out and found the beggar and gave him alms.

The event was to be a seminal one for Francis, and he reflected how commercial interests, even entirely legitimate ones can dull our senses to the plight of the poor; how a preoccupation with acquiring, safeguarding and trading goods can blind us to the needs (and not only the material needs) of those around us. "In his riches, man lacks wisdom" (Ps 49 :12) said the psalmist and Francis went further and saw his neglect of the pauper as an act which perpetuated destitution, and at this early stage Francis' affair with Lady Poverty had begun.

Further reflection on Francis' part suggested that money was inevitable linked with power, and those with money had power which they exercised over those who were poor. Francis recognised that the traders in Assisi who were successful grew richer, but often at the expense of the poor, who become poorer. He had realised profits grew when labour costs were diminished, and he saw that the accumulation of wealth divides societies and even families, and his determination to renounce goods and property grew.

When Francis had recognised the seed of his vocation, he spent some time exploring it and spent at least some time in various Benedictine monasteries. At a personal level it seems he had an unhappy experience at San Verecundo when the monks asked him to leave them. The records give no clue as to what went wrong, and there is suggestion that the monks refused to clothe Francis, i.e. to admit him to their community, but this theory is not substantiated. At any rate it seems Francis was not warmly disposed to the Black Monks at this time. Further at a more fundamental level many of the monasteries were wealthy and well-endowed.

The acquisition, care and tending of monastic land and property, the renting, buying and selling of it was something that had to be done and was something Francis could not reconcile with his own vocation.

In around 1205, having heard a voice inviting him to 'repair my church' Francis lived as a hermit and restored two chapels. Next, at *Santa Maria degli Angeli* at the Potiuncula he was at Mass one day and the words of the Gospel leapt out at him. Jesus' disciples should go out and proclaim the gospel, taking neither gold nor money, no wallet or staff, no shoes or spare tunic, but should preach penance and the arrival of the Kingdom of God. In a flash Francis saw with a new clarity his personal call to continue this apostolic mission, his prayers had been answered and the searching for how he might live out his vocation was ended. Francis was to be an itinerant preacher vowed to poverty.

In the first instance Francis saw this as a private and personal vocation, but as he attracted followers, a new communal dimension arose which in turn prompted questions of how the new fraternity was to live. Francis and his new brothers decided they were to follow their Master, as itinerant preachers, and their renunciation of material goods must go beyond the traditional monastic 'holding goods in common', and must lead to a complete renunciation of goods and property of every kind. The friars were to have a grey woollen tunic with capuche and a cord about their waists and that was it!

Of course, Francis was guided by the Gospels, and his intention was to faithfully follow the example of Jesus himself and that of his first disciples. In the defining Portiuncula Gospel which may be found in Luke 9 (and Matt 10) Jesus sends out the apostles to preach the Kingdom, having given them authority to drive out demons and to cure illness. He tells them to take nothing with them, and to rely on the hospitality of those whom they meet. Michael

Robson observes that "A. Jessop comments that the dominical words to the apostles seemed to Francis to be written in letters of flame; they haunted him waking and sleeping" (Robson p106). He understood them as a direct and personal command from his Divine Master.

As I mentioned above when Francis was joined by new brothers, the first of whom was Bernard, a new dynamic loomed, and decisions about a communal future needed to be made. In search of Divine answers, Francis and Bernard travelled to the church of San Nicola where, after prayer, they made a threefold opening of the Book of the Gospels. The first text was Matt 19:21 where Jesus tells the rich young man that perfection is to be found in giving his possessions to the poor. For Francis and Bernard this was a clear endorsement of their call to poverty, and the renunciation of material goods, for the good of the poor. The second text was Luke 9:3, the Portiuncula text again where the preachers were told to take nothing for their journey, and this seemed to Francis a call to go beyond the normal monastic model of common ownership and resonates with Matt 8:20 where we are told the Son of Man himself had nowhere to lay his head. Jesus himself had no house or home but moved from village to village, house to house owning nothing, and Francis and his companions in imitation of their Master would do likewise.

And the third text was Luke 9:23 where Jesus' followers are warned of future suffering and are told they must daily take up their cross and follow Him. Poverty is in no way an end in itself but is a mode of following Jesus. Poverty is a means by which Francis and his followers could identify themselves intimately with Christ and his salvific work.

It must be said straight away however that Biblical texts need interpretation and contextualisation; they need to be fitted to circumstance in an appropriate way. It seems as though Francis read the scripture particularly literally, and indeed he had to fend off senior clerics such as Cardinal John of St Paul who suggested interpretation and the adoption of a monastic rule. Francis was not a trained theologian and his call, or what we might term the Franciscan founding charism was to take these texts at face value. Two particular things are worthy of note. The first is the suggestion that Francis had invented or discovered a new type of spirituality, a new type of religious order, centred on poverty. This is not strictly true as we find the praise of poverty in Patristic sources. Leo the Great observed that gentleness was often found alongside poverty, whereas pride was more commonly found with riches. Poverty does not seek earthly riches but seeks heavenly riches, and practising poverty was an imitation of Christ himself and the first apostles. In the late fourth century John Chrysostom contrasts poverty and covetousness, depicting poverty as a fair and well-favoured woman. He describes poverty as mild, calm, meek, hating no-one. Francis has then not invented something new, but rediscovered a clear message in the gospel texts and the life of the early church, that had long been ignored or sidelined.

Secondly we may note that the church of the time of Francis was in need of reform. In mediaeval art Jesus and his followers are usually represented bearded and barefoot, whereas many of the bishops, abbots and clergy are depicted in fine clothes and in luxurious surroundings. The church, particularly the monasteries, seemed to be more interested in worldly security, power and wealth than in the salvation of souls. Francis himself was a deacon, not a priest, but his new apostolate recognised the need for reform. There was a growing awareness that the role of the church was not to retreat from society into the silence of monasteries, but to engage with society, preaching the Gospel and caring for the poor. (And in this context we may note S. Anthony was not afraid to be critical of brother priests and even bishops who neglected their sacred duties to their flock).

This change in awareness was prompted by demographic change: as society moved away from farming and the countryside into towns and cities, populations were concentrated and pastoral needs increased. Franciscans and Dominicans too, established themselves in cities and as time went on, in and around universities.

Two final things need to be said. The call to poverty had, for Francis and his followers a profound eschatological dimension. Man enters the world naked and with nothing and will similarly leave the world unable to take anything with him. ("Do not fear when a man grows rich, when the glory of his house increases. He takes nothing with him when he dies, his glory does not follow him below" (Ps 49:16-17) and "Naked I came from my mother's womb and naked I shall return" (Job 1:21)). It is good therefore to be detached from material things, and to recognise that one passes through the world as a pilgrim, on a journey to a higher place. (An idea we have already met in Augustine.) For the Christian, the final aim of life is nothing in this world but is union with God in the next. In this world we are called to be perfect and holy as Jesus was perfect and holy, and whilst there is undoubtedly more than one way of doing this, Francis' radical detachment from material goods is one such way.

Secondly we should recall that Francis' experience in his father's cloth shop was that he failed to help a pauper, and it was his aim and intention throughout his life to help the poor. He believed that he could better help the poor, he could be really on their side as it were, if he were poor himself – the poorest of the poor. Poverty is not an end in itself and but is first and foremost a way of imitating the Saviour and secondly is a precondition for an itinerant life of ministry and service.

Now let us consider the writings of S. Francis, which in all likelihood, S. Anthony would have read. The earliest is

Francis' rudimentary 1208 rule, which no longer survives, but which, according to Thomas of Celano and S. Bonaventure was little more than the passages of the Gospel heard at the chapel of Portiuncula, and an instruction to live the apostolic life; a life centred on chastity, poverty and obedience as in most religious orders. In short, Francis wrote very little in this rule, but his brevity indicates that the brothers were to live wholly according to the Gospel – as literally understood by Francis - especially in its exhortations to poverty. Furthermore, this first rule was written while S Francis himself was still leading and guiding his fledgling order. Francis, not the rule, was the guiding authority, and so there was little or no need to include provision for the future.

By 1220 Francis and his brothers recognised that there was a need for a rule to formalise their growing community, and in particular there was a need for authoritative guidance in Francis' absence. The 1220 rule, which may be regarded as a first draft of the final 1223 rule, is known as the *regula non bullata* as it was not recognised by solemn papal bull. It contained twenty-something sections and was still largely quotation from holy scripture.

The 1220 rule underwent a number of revisions, which were debated and agreed at annual general chapter meetings, and there is some suggestion that these 'debates' were far from amicable, for many of the brothers could not reconcile Francis vision with a growing and sustainable religious order. By 1223 a final version had been agreed and was solemnised by Honorius III, and this is the definitive version of the Franciscan rule which is in use today. It is slightly shorter than its 1220 predecessor, consisting of a mere twelve sections, and it omits some of Francis' stricter injunctions (c.f. Robson p146). For those who study religious rules there is much that could be said about the evolution and content of the 1223 rule, but I want to focus upon three particular points that seem to me to be most notable and which contrast with the rule of S. Augustine considered above.

Whereas Augustine talks of community, Francis talks of family. It seems he (Francis) does not want to formulate a canonical constitution but that he has a new ideal. The relationships between the brothers should not be governed by rights and obligations but should be based – as in a family – on love. He writes "And wherever brothers meet one another, let them act like members of a common family....for if a mother loves and cares for her carnal son, how much more should one love and care for his spiritual son?" (Rule chap VI). This general precept is particularly fleshed out in the case of a brother who is ill "let the brothers serve him as they themselves would like to be served" (ibid.).

And similarly if brothers sin – and the rule says mortally rather than venially – they should have recourse to a priest who "should mercifully prescribe a penance for them" (chap VII). The emphasis here is upon mercy, and the return of the errant brother to the fold. There should not be anger or upset as these are contrary to love. Again he writes "ministers should receive them [brothers] lovingly and generously and treat them so intimately that the brothers can speak and act as lords do with their servants" (chap. X).

Unsurprisingly Francis is quite explicit about the brothers' observance of holy poverty. He says they should appropriate nothing for themselves, and particularly they should not have a house, being content to be pilgrims in the world "serving God in poverty and humility" (chap VI). Concerning clothes, the new brother in his novitiate is to have "two tunics with hoods, belt and trousers, and a chaperon reaching down to the belt" (chap II). After a year of probation a brother received into the order and vowed to obedience should have just one tunic with hood and a spare without a hood if they wish it. Again those who must, may wear sandals, but clearly Francis' original intention was that the brothers would go barefoot.

Finally Francis as adamant that the brothers should not receive money, either as a gift or as payment for work. He says of work, "As payment for their labour let them receive that which is necessary for themselves and their brothers, but not money" (chap V). They should always seek after holiest poverty.

With this in mind the brothers are to beg for their essential necessities, or as Francis says "they should go confidently after alms" (chap VI). They should not be ashamed or embarrassed to be poor, or to receive alms for in so doing they are imitating the Master who himself was made poor (by God) in this world for us. By abandoning the riches of the world the friars may focus on the riches of heaven. Francis writes "poverty which has made you, my dearest brothers, heirs and kings of the kingdom of heaven, poor in things but rich in virtues" (ibid).

Finally Francis, draws the brothers' attention to prayer. Firstly he does so in a rather legalistic way, prescribing the divine office in accord with the Roman rite for clerics and a collection of '*Pater Nosters*' for each liturgical hour (totalling seventy-six per day!) to be said by laymen. He also says, somewhat abruptly "They should also pray for the dead" (chap III).

Later we get a little more of the true sense of Franciscan prayer, for despite all outward observances "above all they should wish to have the spirit of the Lord working within them, and that they should pray to him constantly with a pure heart" (ibid chap X). Prayer then is to be a regular recitation of verbal prayers, but additionally it is to be a constant disposition. It is to be a recognition of the Lord working with and through them, and it is to be a dedication to the furtherance of that indwelling Divine will.

Francis was not an academic and not a 'big writer', by his own admission, he considered himself as an *idiota,* unlettered in both clerical and secular learning. The rule is short, some twelve brief 'chapters' which in reality are little more than a paragraph or two each. It is a summary in the briefest form of the life that Francis would have *shown* to his brothers, and of itself it is perhaps not a very illuminating document. Despite the compassion in the rule, it seems, necessarily, rather legalistic and terse. The Canticle of Brother Sun is in marked contrast to this.

Francis wrote the Canticle of Brother Sun in the summer or autumn of 1225, when, we are told, he felt relieved of a heavy spiritual burden, and he sang the song to Sister Clare and her companions, although we no longer have any associated tune. In a modern translation it is a poem of some thirty-one lines. It is first and foremost a hymn of praise to the Lord, in thanksgiving for all creation, but it has a certain freshness and vibrancy even if the rhyme and metre sound naïve to the modern ear.

Underlying the poem is Francis' respect for the whole of the created order, and the recognition that it is divinely created and has a divine end. He wished to make all of creation aware of its Divine origins and its Divine end, and he was genuinely filled with awe and wonder and the natural order, especially the sun, the moon and the stars. With an uncanny prescience he saw a unity in the created order and referred to the constellations and the elements as brother and sister. "Praised be, Thou my Lord for Brother Sun,....Sister Moon, ..Brother Wind...and Sister Water" (Canticle, Karrer p261). He also refers to mother earth and movingly to brother bodily death, from whom no man can ever escape.

Francis' poem is perhaps based on the hymn of the three young men in the furnace in Daniel 3, and is perhaps a recognition that absolute trust in God is the relief of all our burdens. Indeed the trust of the three young men saved them from the furnace even when it had been heated "seven times more than it was wont to be heated" (Dan 3:19). Maybe too the canticle is a realisation that trust in God would have prevented Francis' own burden – whatever it was.

Finally Francis wrote a Testament or final exhortation to his brothers, between May and September 1226, and it is perhaps the finest or purest culmination or distillation of his ideas. Although it reads like the rule, it does not have its canonical status; Francis himself writes "And do not let the brothers say 'this is another Rule' because this is a reminder, an admonition and an exhortation" (Testament, Karrer p275). Additionally Pope Gregory IX in the constitution *Quo elongati* of 1230 confirmed the Testament was not binding, for it lacked the sanction of the general chapter.

Reading the Testament we find a brief history of Francis' call and the development of his understanding of it. Also we find a declaration of Francis' deep respect for the clergy. He writes "I look upon them as my masters" because in a sacramental way they carry the image of Christ himself, and hence they alone can offer the sacrifice of the Mass and administer His most holy Body and Blood. Moreover "theologians and those that announce the most holy words of God" are to be honoured and venerated too.

Overall perhaps we find in the Testament a call to sanctity, and an injunction to live according to the rule of the Holy Gospel. For Francis this is characterised primarily by a call to poverty which we have already discussed, but Francis re-asserts that his followers are to be as pilgrims in the world, "taking shelter like wanderers and strangers" (ibid).

The other theme that particularly emerges is a call to obedience. There are two dimensions to this. Firstly there is a call to obey the Minister General of the Order and his deputies and here we can see Francis' provision to ensure the stability and good conduct of his fledgling Order. Also he admonishes the ministers and custodians themselves to add nothing to his words and take nothing away. He says they "shall make no gloss on the Rule" (ibid) which they shall follow simply and humbly as Francis himself has done.

Secondly as we have identified an eschatological dimension to Francis understanding of poverty, surely there is a Christological dimension to the insistence on obedience. Christ came not to be served but to serve and was obedient even unto death, death on a cross. Obedience does not simply serve earthly ends, although it does that, it also serves a Divine end, and Francis asserts the "whoever shall observe these things, will be filled with the blessing of the highest Heavenly Father in heaven" (Karrer p276). Sanctity derives from imitating Christ, and for Francis this is to be understood as a call to poverty and obedience.

This is a message that Anthony cannot fail to have received, but given his background as an Augustinian Canon, and his first acquaintance with the friars in Coimbra, it is surely a message that would have come as little surprise to him, and would have found a ready home in his spirituality. It is however worth noting that the simplicity of Francis' thinking and writing was at marked odds with Anthony's intellectual approach, and Francis insistence that there should be no gloss on his Rule, that is, that it should be understood literally and without any kind of interpretation, is an insistence with which Anthony may have struggled.

Finally, as I have suggested above it will be convenient to consider the call to martyrdom as a Franciscan influence on S. Anthony although this call is not uniquely Franciscan, but given the influence this notion had upon Anthony and given Francis himself seems to have sought martyrdom it will be convenient to consider it here.

Firstly, when Anthony was about seventeen years old he joined the priory of *São*

Vicente in Lisbon which was a royal foundation, dedicated to St Vincent of Zaragoza. This dedication is immediately significant for Vincent was a deacon to Bishop Valerius in Zaragoza at the very end of the third century and was martyred under Diocletian in 304. His martyrdom was particularly graphically narrated by Prudentius and St Augustine preached sermons about him. It would be foolish to attribute too much influence on the young Anthony, but the manner of the death of his first patron cannot have escaped him, and veneration of martyrs particularly Vincent, would not have passed him by particularly if some of St Vincent's relics are to be found in Lisbon.

Secondly, Augustine says little about martyrdom, because of the apologetic nature of his writing and the absence of any major persecution of the church at Augustine's time. The persecutions of the early church were largely over and the call to convert Muslims had not yet begun (as there were no Muslims then!). Nevertheless Augustine recognised the (liturgical) cult of the martyrs and we may assume Anthony, in his reading of Augustine, would have been aware of this too. For example in his sermon for the feast of S. Laurence (deacon and martyr, 10 August) S. Augustine points out that as a deacon, Laurence administered Christ's blood to the faithful, and recognizing the Lord's self-giving, gave himself too in imitation of his Master. He goes on "Brethren, let us imitate Laurence if we truly love Christ. We cannot show a better proof of our love than by imitating him" (Augustine's sermon for the feast of S. Laurence).

Thirdly, and perhaps most significantly Anthony would certainly have been involved in the events surrounding the return of the five Franciscan protomartyrs from Morocco to Coimbra. They initially travelled to Morocco via Coimbra, where they had received the support of Queen Urraca. They travelled around Morocco preaching Christianity, but their message was not well received and having ignored a number of injunctions to remain silent, finally on 16 January 1220 they were all martyred. Their bodies were returned to Coimbra, and as the Franciscan house in Coimbra was too small to house the bodies, the five were interred in the cloister of the monastery of *Santa Cruz*, burial site of Portuguese kings. Anthony would certainly have attended the liturgies surrounding these events, and could not have failed to be moved by them. Indeed the *Assidua* asserts "Later when Peter, the Lord Infante, brought from Morocco the relics of the holy Franciscan martyrs.......He used to say within his heart 'If only the Most High would deign to make me share in the crown of his holy martyrs! If only the executioner's sword would strike me as I, on bended knee, offer Him my neck for the name of Jesus!'....He would silently say these and similar things to himself" (*Assidua* p22).

Fourthly, and probably later than the events described above, in Sicily or Assisi perhaps, Anthony would have learnt more of Francis' own desire to be martyred. When Francis grew up in Assisi were there was a veneration of martyrs, particularly *San Giorgio* who died in the crusades and San Rufino (martyred 238) who was the patron saint of Assisi and to whom the cathedral was dedicated. Francis also had a devotion to S. John the Baptist (c.f. Robson p25) and Thomas of Celano believed that there was in Francis, a continuity between his early attempts to be a soldier and a knight, and his later understanding of being a soldier of Christ. In medieval times martyrdom was a near perfect identification with the crucifixion of Jesus himself, and was therefore a highly elevated Franciscan ideal.

Indeed Francis risked his own life, on three missionary journeys. Around 1212 he made his first attempt to visit the Holy Land but contrary winds blew him off course. He made a second attempt some years later but illness prevented him preaching. Finally in 1219 he reached Syria and attempted dialogue with the Muslim leaders in the midst of battles with the crusaders. Francis preached with some success and the earliest sources speak of his great courage, but also his respectfulness and courtesy.

Francis was not martyred, but it is said that when he heard of the death of the protomartyrs he exclaimed "Now I can truly say that I have five real lesser brethren" and a brief chapter concerning those who go among the Saracens and other Infidels *(De euntibus inter saracenos et alios infideles)* was included in the 1223 Rule.

All in all then, Anthony would have been exposed to a number of influences that would have inclined him towards martyrdom. However as we know this was not to be Anthony's fate and perhaps 'martyrdom' as an influence had more effect on his actions than his writings and intellectual development. Nevertheless, I often think that by the time Anthony reached the hermitage at *Montepaulo* to say Mass for five lay brothers, and to tend the kitchen with his plans for preaching in Morocco in tatters and his desire for martyrdom unrealised (not to mention his academic life abandoned), he must have reflected at length on Divine providence and his own life. In this sense, in the sense of how his own plans were *not* fulfilled, and how he had to learn utter dependence on God, the influence of the cult of the martyr upon S. Anthony is perhaps one of the most powerful and far-reaching.

To conclude then, Anthony was a well-versed and schooled Augustinian, who came under the influence of the nascent Franciscan Order. We must be careful not to attribute too much 'Franciscan theology' to Anthony, but we can be fairly certain that Anthony would have received the fundamental message of poverty, the message to be found in Francis' writings, especially his rule, and it has been convenient to consider here the cult of the martyr which clearly influenced Anthony too. Further as Anthony met more Franciscans in Sicily, Assisi and elsewhere he would have engaged more with emergent Franciscan ideals, and his own thought would have taken an increasingly Franciscan turn.

This twin set of influences puts Anthony in a unique or near unique position at that time in the Franciscan Order, and in some ways the depth of Anthony's Augustinian upbringing may be seen as a balance and a stabilising force to counter the fervour of enthusiasm in the new Franciscan Order. In particular Anthony's understanding of poverty, his commitment to study and his recognition that work and prayer were not antagonistic but go hand in hand in the Christian life were, as we shall see, to have far reaching effects.

As a brief aside it seems highly significant to me that the founder of the other great mediaeval preaching order, the Order of Preachers or Dominicans was also a schooled Augustinian who left his cloister to preach the Gospel. S. Dominic was born in 1170 in Spain, and after study at Palencia University he became a canon at Osma Cathedral, living in community under the rule of S. Augustine. By the turn of the century Dominic was prior of the community.

Travelling in France Dominic met the heresy of the Cathars and was duly asked by Pope Honorius III to join a team to preach to the heretics and to establish orthodoxy; he continued to wear the habit of a regular Augustinian canon and to follow the Augustinian rule. Being a wandering preacher was not without its canonical problems and three times Dominic was invited to become a bishop but on each occasion he declined. As time went on a group of followers surrounded Dominic, and he began to envisage a body of men who would study and contemplate, but who would also preach.

Here is not the place to rehearse the origins of the Order of Preachers but suffice to say that by 1216, the first Dominican community had been established and the fledgling order, living a vowed life under the rule of S. Augustine had received papal approval.

Dominic and his brothers were of course vowed to poverty, but they did not have the problems of interpretation that beset the Franciscans, and from the start academic study (centred upon universities) and the religious life went hand in hand. Missionary zeal and the life of the preacher was founded upon, or perhaps better emerged from a firm theological foundation, centred on a common Augustinian life, where study and the practice of virtue were considered as opposite sides of the same coin.

Dominic was a founder and lived until he was 51, whereas Anthony was not a founder and died at the age of 36, but the similarities are striking, and the life of preaching and teaching emerging from an Augustinian discipline is not insignificant. Having said that there were many other successful Dominicans and Franciscans who did not have Augustinian backgrounds, so I do not want to overstate the significance of this similarity, but I do think it is worthy of note, and in particular I think that Anthony is better understood when the twin influences of Augustine and Francis are recognised.

Section Two

S. Anthony's Preaching and Teaching

2.1   S. Anthony and Sacred Scripture

Like most of those who went before him, S. Anthony's theology was first and foremost centred on Holy Scripture. We know from the earliest sources that Anthony travelled around preaching the Gospel, and teaching not only the people, but at S. Francis' specific injunction, his brother friars too.

S. Anthony's extant writings also point to this focus on the Bible. Anthony did not write theological treatises or a Summa of theology, but left a series of sermons, commenting week by week on Holy Scripture, as found in the lectionary of the church. Furthermore even the most cursory glance at these writings indicate a huge familiarity with the Bible and the sermons as a whole contain over six thousand biblical references from whole of the Old and the New Testaments. Indeed some traditions suggest that S. Anthony knew the Bible by heart.

Similar traditions are found in the iconography of S. Anthony who is almost always portrayed with a book – the

Bible. Often Anthony is portrayed with the Christ child, either in his arms or sitting on the Bible, which is a kind of pun and underlines Anthony's devotion and love both of the word of God and the Word of God (incarnate).

For Anthony then, theology was biblical theology and as Jarmak says "Saint Anthony defines theology as 'the knowledge of Sacred Scripture' the font and source of all wisdom" (Jarmak p23). He goes on to say that "Philosophy, philology and natural sciences and all other studies have their foundation and raison d'être in Scripture, that is in theology" (ibid). S. Anthony himself is explicit in his sermon for the Second Sunday after Easter: considering the verse "Sing unto the Lord a new Song" (Ps 95:1) he writes that "All worldly knowledge how to make money is the 'old song', the knowledge of Babylon. Only theology is the 'new song' sweetly sounding in the Lord's ear and renewing the soul" (Spilsbury I p280). The following week – the third Sunday after Easter - he says "O man take to yourself this book that you may drive out your barrenness with its riches, your neediness with its abundance" (ibid p306).

But we get a little ahead of ourselves. The sermons that Anthony wrote towards the end of his life are not sermons in the modern sense. They are *sermones* or outlines of sermons, written as instruction for his brother friars, as a sort of mediaeval text book for preachers, containing skeleton sermons, notes and examples. No doubt many were based on sermons that Anthony actually preached, but the written text is certainly not a verbatim record. Anthony himself referred to his text as his *Opus*, or *Opus Evangeliorum* which is perhaps best rendered as commentary on the Gospels. This commentary falls into two sections which were probably written in different places and at different times.

The first section is of Sunday sermons (*Sermones Dominicales*). This section was probably written in Limoges, where Anthony was Custos, around 1226 (c.f. Huber p47) and is a collection of some fifty sermons for the Sundays of the church year. The second section, which remains unfinished, was probably written in Padua between 1229 and 1230 and consists of four Marian sermons and some fifteen sermons for feast days and festivals.

We may ask what was Anthony's intention in his writings and how did he bring this about? Anthony himself provides us with the answer to the first question in his general prologue. His aim is to harmonise the Sunday Gospel with the Epistle of the day, the Gradual and lessons from the breviary (i.e. the Old Testament). He imagines his sermons as a chariot (*quadriga*) and says "And note that as on a chariot there are four wheels, so in this work four matters are dealt with, namely the Lord's Gospels, the history of the Old Testament as it is read in church, the Introit and the Epistle of the Sunday Mass. I have collected together and concorded each of these, as Divine grace has granted and as far as my slender and paltry knowledge allows" (prologue 5, Spilsbury I p4).

The concordances of which Anthony speaks are connections or links, patterns and themes. Sometimes these may be relatively straightforward such as when Anthony relates the seven days of creation in the Old Testament to the seven articles of faith from the New Testament (the birth, baptism, passion, resurrection and ascension of Christ, the mission of the Holy Spirit and the final judgement) on Septuagesima Sunday. But at other times (e.g. Sexagesima) Anthony seems almost obscure to the modern reader as for example where he concords the gospel passage where a farmer goes out to sow some seed (Lk 8:54) with God's instruction to Noah to build the ark of timber covered inside and out with pitch (Gen 6:14). Anthony's link is that as the Father tells the Son to go out and sow seed – i.e. establish the Church, so the ark is to be covered with the 'pitch' of saints on the inside and the pitch of mercy and love on the outside. The lesson here is to remember that Anthony was pre scholastic, and did not employ modern methods of exegesis. Like all historical authors he must be understood in the age in which he wrote.

A further point to add is that in mediaeval times the task of preaching was first and foremost an episcopal task. As churches grew the bishops deputed this task firstly to their priests and then (indirectly) to the emerging preaching orders. The Fourth Lateran council (1215) recognised that the preaching role of the bishop had to be extended if the church was to be effective. Lateran IV was also concerned particularly with pastoral practice and directed preachers to encourage the faithful in word and deed. This encouragement was particularly to confess their sins to a priest at least once a year, and to receive the sacrament of Holy Communion at Easter time. In the sermons then, the parallels and concordances are not just an academic exercise, but are designed to lead to practical and moral guidance. In other words, Anthony's sermons are not just an academic exercise, they have a pastoral message too, and this is something which should not be overlooked.

Now let us turn to the method that Anthony used to build his chariot, to fashion and form his concordances. Anthony was brought up and trained as an Augustinian and as we have already seen Augustine embraced the Alexandrian exegetical position, recognising multiple meanings in a given text. The roots of this position lie in the Platonism of Philo, which suggested that 'beneath' the obvious meaning there was a spiritual meaning, which told of God. This position was accepted by Origen, one of the masters of the Alexandrian school, and in turn by Augustine. This is not to say that Anthony would not have been aware of the Antiochene school, indeed he almost certainly would have been, but this was not as dominant in the west and indeed some Antiochenes were suspected of Christological heresies.

Anthony's approach then was a method of exegesis transmitted to him via Augustine that recognised both a literal meaning and a spiritual meaning in a text. The spiritual meaning in turn can be split into several subdivisions; the allegorical, the moral and the anagogical. In his sermon for the ninth Sunday after Pentecost, Anthony quotes from the book of proverbs and develops the theme that as milk comes from two breasts – which represent the Old and New Testaments – so in turn from this milk other products may be made. "Note that milk is made up of three elements. First there is the watery matter, the whey. Second the curds from which cheese is made. The third is butter. The whey is the historical meaning, the cheese is allegory, the butter is morality" (Spilsbury II p208).

In other words firstly we have a literal sense, and Anthony does not neglect this. Indeed when matters of Catholic Dogma are under consideration, he stresses the literal truth of the text. We find this particularly when he refers to texts concerning the Blessed Virgin Mary, the Incarnation, the Trinity, the Blessed Eucharist etc. Indeed in proclaiming Anthony a Doctor of the Church, Pope Pius XII declared that he who peruses Anthony's sermons will find (among other things) "a most experienced exegete in the interpretation of Sacred Scriptures, a deep theologian in the elucidation of dogmatic truths" (Exulta Lusitania Felix c.f. Huber p76).

For example, S. Anthony reflects on the name of Jesus to teach us about the Incarnation. He says "The name 'Jesus' has two syllables and five letters, three vowels and two consonants. Two syllables because Jesus has two natures, divine and human...two syllables in one name, because there are two natures in this one Person" (Spilsbury IV p66). He goes on to add that the three vowels are the three persons of the trinity and the two consonant represent the body and soul of a person, and in Jesus these are conjoined. Jesus is both truly God and truly man. Of course Anthony does not see a causal link here (between spelling and theology!), but understanding the sermons as a preacher's guidebook, he develops these connections as a kind of 'aide-memoir' to ensure his readers preach with rigour and orthodoxy.

Again on the Eucharist, Anthony's guidance to the preacher underlines Church teaching. Quoting in parts he writes "It is firmly to be believed and confessed with the mouth, that the very body which the virgin bore, which hung in the cross and lay in the tomb, which rose the third day and ascended to the right hand of the Father in heaven: this body the church truly makes daily and gives to her faithful. At the words: *this is my body*, bread is transubstantiated into the body of Christ" (Spilsbury IV p185).

Moreover Anthony's sermons suggest he was certainly aware of the variations that occur in different parts of the Bible, especially in the gospel narratives. As Rohr says (Rohr p44) Anthony may not have been aware of all the problems of exegesis that modern scholars have identified, but there is an attempt on Anthony's part to reconcile apparent differences. For example in Matthew and Mark's gospels Mary Magdalen anoints the head of Jesus with precious ointment (Matt 26:7, Mk14:3), whereas in John's account she anoints his feet (John 12:3). Whilst Anthony does not offer any type of explanation of this problem he reconciles the accounts by saying Mary anointed Christ's head *and* his feet (c.f. Sermon for Palm Sunday, Spilsbury I p212) and adds the explanation or teaching device, that in so doing Mary anoints the head of Jesus' divinity and the feet of his humanity.

Secondly then we have a spiritual sense, and this may be allegorical, moral (tropological) or anagogical. The allegorical sense is Anthony's cheese, and it is a product of the milk, i.e. the allegorical sense is derived from the literal sense of scripture. Expressing the same thing in another way, he writes ""The earth which of itself brings forth fruit, first the blade and then the ear, afterwards the full corn on the ear" (Mk 4:28). By the blade we understand the allegorical sense of scripture which builds up faith" (Spilsbury I p1).

In the thirteenth century the allegorical sense of scripture was the way in which an event in the Old Testament prefigured an event in the New. The allegory first and foremost points to the centrality of Christ, who is foretold in the Old Testament and fully realised in the New, but also to a lesser degree things such as Noah's Ark and Jerusalem may be understood allegorically to point to the establishment of the church in the New Testament.

Anthony's allegorical connections are too many to list but as an example he picks up on the allegory of the brazen serpent, which is mentioned by Christ himself (John 3:14). The brazen serpent made by Moses in Numbers 21 prefigures Christ, both because bronze indicates divinity since it is not consumed in time, and the exaltation of the serpent represents Christ lifted up upon the cross (c.f. Spilsbury IV p225). Similarly, as Elisha raises the dead child in 2 Kings 4 by bowing himself down over the child, so Christ in his incarnation bows himself over humanity and restores it to full faith and life (c.f. Spilsbury IV p25).

For Anthony, the key to many of these allegorical connections is some etymological or philological link. For example Anthony writes "Scholars say the name David means 'merciful' others that it means 'strong-armed', or else 'desirable in appearance'. David then stands for the Son of God, Jesus Christ, who was merciful in his incarnation, strong-armed in his passions and who will be desirable for us to behold in eternal blessedness" (Prologue, Spilsbury I p2).

In much of this S. Anthony was influenced by the Church Fathers, particularly S. Jerome and S. Isidore, whom he quotes directly six times. Anthony may well have been drawn to Isidore on account of him being a fellow Iberian, or perhaps his manuscripts may have been particularly readily available to Anthony. Isidore stressed the importance of study of the Bible, remarking that when we pray it is we who talk to God, but when we read holy scripture we allow God to speak to us. Isidore's most famous work the *Etymologiae* was a kind of mediaeval encyclopaedia, which contained not only science and rhetoric but theological matters too.

In contrast to some biographers, Rohr suggests that S. Anthony's grasp of ancient languages such as Greek, Hebrew and Syriac, upon which many of these etymological derivations come, may have been limited and perhaps Anthony relies on Jerome, Isidore *et al.* for these linguistic connections. For example, Anthony's interpretation of *diabolus* meaning rushing downwards (twenty-third Sunday after Pentecost) may also be found in both Isidore and Jerome. Other examples may be given, but if Anthony's command of ancient languages was limited then we have a ready explanation of Anthony's quite extensive use of Isidore and Jerome (see Rohr p31-33).

The third sense of scripture (or the second product of the literal sense) is its moral sense. At the time of S. Anthony there was a development in the moral exegesis of scripture, and a focus on moral issues, and Anthony certainly saw holy scripture as the basis of moral teaching. Peter Comestor who was a Victorine Canon was particularly noteworthy in promoting biblical-moral exegesis, and is often quoted by S. Anthony (c.f. Marcil p37). Additionally as I have already mentioned the fourth Lateran Council called for reform in the Church and in particular a call to renewed penance and sacramental confession. Anthony's pages are full of moral encouragement, calls for repentance and confession.

Let us consider a couple of examples of moral interpretation. In his sermon for the first Sunday after Easter Anthony considers the verse "when it was late the same day..." (Jn 20:19) and then concords it with a passage from the Acts of the Apostles, where S. Peter quotes the prophet Joel: "I will show wonders in the heaven above and signs in the earth beneath, blood and fire and vapour of smoke. The sun shall be turned into darkness and the moon into blood" (Acts 2:19-20). Anthony goes on to say "morally, blood stands for mortification of the flesh, fire for the ardour of charity and the vapour of smoke for compunction of heart. The Lord gives these signs 'in heaven' (that is, in the just) and 'on earth' (in sinners)" (Spilsbury I p255).

Again in his sermon for the nineteenth Sunday after Pentecost, Anthony considers the departure of Abraham from Egypt (Gen 13) with all his possessions: sheep cattle, gold and so on. Anthony interprets Egypt as moral darkness or misery (c.f. Spilsbury III p48) and Abraham's departure from Egypt represents the penitent soul leaving the darkness of sin. Further there can be no half measures and as Abraham takes *all* his household and possessions, so our moral reform must be complete. We reject sin entirely, and depart from it utterly to enter unconditionally into Bethel – 'the house of God' (ibid).

It is worth noting that in the sermons generally, Anthony does not seem to teach about what we might think of as particular moral issues, he doesn't get involved in contentious moral debate. Rather he seems to take an understanding of morals for granted, and his sense of moral teaching is a teaching of a moral attitude, a way of living and an insistence that we turn our backs on sin and embrace virtue – reject darkness and enter the light. There are exceptions of course, and Anthony does teach of the purpose of matrimony and the duties that marriage entails. He distinguishes the nature of venial and mortal sins and of their specific and numerical distinctions, and he teaches of the sanctity and seal of the confessional (c.f. Huber p80).

Finally the anagogical sense of scripture, although explored less by S. Anthony than the other spiritual senses points towards an eternal meaning or final end, as Rohr has it: a place of "perfect happiness enjoyed by the angels and the Church triumphant in heaven" (Rohr p 61). Anthony often interprets passages from the Old Testament in this way and in particular he interprets texts concerning Jerusalem and the Temple on the one hand, and texts concerning banquets and feasts on the other as pointing towards the beatific vision of the Church in heaven.

For example in the sermon for the fifteenth Sunday after Pentecost, Anthony considers Tobit's Jerusalem, "built up with sapphires and emeralds and precious stones; thy walls and towers and battlements with pure gold. And the streets of Jerusalem shall be paved with beryl and carbuncle and stones of Ophir" (Tob 13:16, 17). Having considered allegorical and moral interpretations of this text, Anthony says that anagogically "The sapphire stands for contemplation of the inexpressible Trinity and Unity. Emerald, which transforms the eyes, represents the joyful vision of the whole triumphant Church. The precious stone is the eternal fulfilment of heavenly joy" (Spilsbury II p420).

Considering banquets Anthony says that the Lord has prepared three wedding feasts for us. Firstly of union – "Celebrated in the temple of the blessed virgin; the second is daily celebrated in the temple of the faithful soul; the third will be celebrated in the temple of heavenly glory (Spilsbury III p68). He goes on to say Jesus is the groom who will welcome his bride, the church, to the wedding feast. Whereas the church now lives by faith and hope, "in a little while [she] will celebrate the marriage with her bridegroom" (ibid p70) in heaven.

Anthony goes on to say that for various reasons there are many who do not accept the Lord's generous invitation, and who are too preoccupied with the business of this earth. But the one who does accept it keeps careful watch over his conduct, flees the values of the world and perceives the will of God. He does not act like a fool but the prudent man who can taste and see how gracious the Lord is. Anthony ends this section as he often does with a prayer, summing up his previous remarks "We ask you then, Lord Jesus Christ, to make us come in faith and humility to the wedding feast of your Incarnation; to celebrate the marriage of penitence whereby we may attend the wedding of heavenly glory. Grant this, you who are blessed for ever. Amen" (Spilsbury III p 75).

By way of conclusion I think four things may be said. Firstly that there is little doubt that Anthony knew the Bible extremely well; he had obviously studied it very closely and in a significant sense he had made the text of the Bible his own. Secondly as we have seen Anthony followed the prevailing wisdom of the time and understood and interpreted this text at four distinct levels, drawing out a number of senses or meanings from the same verbal text. Thirdly Anthony based all his teachings on Holy Scripture, no doubt when he preached himself, but also in providing a textbook for his brothers he clearly drew his doctrinal and moral teaching directly from the words of scripture. And fourthly and finally, Anthony integrated his biblical teaching with prayer.

When S. Francis wrote to Anthony to appoint him as Franciscan teacher in Bologna, he instructed him to teach sacred theology so long as the spirit of prayer and devotion of the brethren was not extinguished. In the prayers that are regularly to be found in the sermons we see Anthony to have obeyed Francis, and that for Anthony study of the Bible and prayer are all one, or perhaps better are the opposite sides of the same coin: prayer enabling and enhancing study as study deepens and enriches the life of prayer.

But if we look at Anthony's sacred theology and understanding of prayer a little more closely what do we find? What are the salient or distinctive characteristics of S.

Anthony's theology and understanding of spirituality? It is to these questions that we now turn.

2.2   Christology

Concerning Anthony's Christology, there seems to be an argument, or at least an assumption something along the following lines. As S. Francis was trying to discern his vocation he performed a threefold opening of the gospels and interpreted his findings that he should follow Christ in poverty, without any security, preaching the good news in an itinerant manner. Francis tried to imitate Christ's earthly life as closely as he could, and as such was particularly devoted to Christ in his incarnation, and developed a new kind of spirituality that focussed in a particular way on the humanity of the second person of the Trinity. The argument or suggestion then tends to be that, "as a follower of S. Francis of Assisi, Anthony was devoted above all to the incarnate Christ" (Nugent p24).

It seems to me that this kind of inference is at best misleading and at worst simply untrue. Firstly, while S. Francis undoubtedly strove to imitate Christ in a particular way, as he found Him in the gospels, Francis was a relatively unlettered and unsophisticated man (by his own admission), and the suggestion that he could have transformed his random openings of the book of the gospels into a coherent Christological position seems unlikely to me. Secondly, even if Francis had done this, given the dates that I discussed at the beginning of section 1.2 it seems highly unlikely that this position could have been reliably transmitted to S. Anthony, or that he could have received the influence of a 'new Franciscan spirituality'. And thirdly there are alternative reasons which are in themselves more convincing to explain why Christology is at the heart of S. Anthony's theology. It seems to me much more likely that S. Anthony *contributed* to a developing Franciscan Christocentric spirituality than he was influenced by it.

Firstly, as we have seen Anthony's intellectual focus was on holy scripture, and was therefore a focus on the good news of Jesus Christ as found in the new testament and an understanding of the Old Testament as the preparation of this. Through his numerous concordances and allegorical interpretations he shows how the whole of holy writ points to and concerns God's plan for salvation centred on the life, death and resurrection of Jesus Christ. In his sermon for Sexagesima he declares "The God of the new testament is one and the same as the God of the old, and is indeed Jesus Christ the Son of God" (Spilsbury I p35).

Secondly, Anthony was renowned for his preaching to the heretics and was indeed known as *malleus haereticorum* or hammer of the heretics. Who were these heretics? Principally they were followers of variants of ancient Manichaeism, who were known as Albigensians in southern France and Cathari in Italy. They were essentially dualists who believed that God had created the spiritual realm, whereas God's adversary had created the material world including human bodies. The indwelling of a mind and a soul in a body gave life to the whole, but was also the essence of original sin. Therefore, to these heretics, it was unreasonable that the Divine Word would take on a human body, and they developed ingenious if fanciful theories about the incarnation. Crucially, they rejected the orthodox position of the Church. If Anthony was to counter the heretics with orthodox teaching about the person of Christ, little wonder then that he had a well-formed Christology!

Further as Michael Robson points out (Robson p171) many of the heretics were well-educated and articulate and theological debate of the time was often both public and keenly contested. Lengthy debates were sometimes staged and so for Anthony to engage with the heretics he would have had to employ skills of rhetoric and debate, but also he would have to have been absolutely on top of his game – Christologically speaking.

Thirdly and finally as we have already mentioned Anthony was influenced to some extent by Hugh of S. Victor and others from the Paris school. They sought wisdom through a study of Wisdom Himself. In other words the accumulation of knowledge and wisdom was not a pure intellectual activity (an empty desire) but was directed towards a divine end. Knowledge and wisdom were ultimately knowledge and wisdom of Christ who is all Knowledge and Wisdom. "The need for the restoration of the relationship between God and fallen humanity through union with this Wisdom is the basis for the Victorine view of education and its interest in biblical exegesis. The Christocentric strain in the Victorines would later be carried on in the Franciscan school….." (Marcil p34).

In other words Anthony is not notably Christocentric in his outlook and teaching, *because* of following S. Francis, but because of his understanding of the Bible, because of the academic tradition in which he was schooled and because of a need to counter widespread heresies, which tended to deviate from orthodox teaching about the person of Christ. These are more convincing reasons for S. Anthony's Christological focus. What are the distinctive strands in this teaching?

Although the feast of Christ the King was not formally instituted until 1925 (by Pope Pius XI) the notion of the kingship of Christ appears regularly in scripture and is discussed by many fathers and doctors of the church. Anthony of Padua regularly refers to Christ as a king, and to the mystery of his eternal kingship. Many, but not all, of these scriptural references are centred on the narrative of the passion.

As Christ entered Jerusalem, Anthony reflects that the prophecies of Zechariah and Jeremiah are fulfilled. "Look your king is approaching.....humble and riding on a donkey" (Zech 9:9) and "Who would not revere you, king of nations" (Jer 10:7). Anthony observes that as Christ was wrapped in swaddling clothes at his birth, these were his kingly purple, but his is not a kingship of power and fear, but a kingship of justice and piety, as emphasised by the mode of his entry into Jerusalem. "Your king is just, in respect of justice, rendering to each according to his works. He is meek, and a redeemer, with respect to piety" (Sermon for Palm Sunday, Spilsbury I p218).

This theme is continued in Anthony's reflection on the passion and he sees an irony in the determination of the Jews to strip Christ of his kingship, (seen symbolically in the stripping of Christ of his clothes) and yet the irony is that they then dressed him in purple and put a crown upon his head, thus proclaiming the very kingship they sought to deny. Additionally Anthony says "for after crown and purple he lacked only a sceptre and this he took when he went out, bearing his cross" (ibid). On the twenty-second Sunday after Pentecost Anthony makes the point again, "This man who is a king is Jesus Christ, man in his humanity, king in his divinity; man in his nativity, king in his passion, wherein he had the regalia proper to a king: crown, purple and sceptre" (Spilsbury III p119). The irony is further underlined by the inscription they placed above Him on the cross "Jesus the Nazarene, King of the Jews" (John 19:19).

The repentant thief asks Jesus to remember him *in his kingdom*, and Anthony notes that this request bears the mark of a holy confessor inspired by the virtues of faith hope and charity, which are to be contrasted at this stage with S. Peter who denied Christ earlier the same morning. Anthony also concords the crucifixion with the story of Joseph imprisoned between the cup-bearer and the baker of the king of Egypt (Gen 40). The baker concords with the prisoner who taunts

Christ, and is led to the gallows; whereas the cup-bearer who concords with the repentant thief "leave[s] prison for the king's palace" (Spilsbury I p154). The concordance with Christ's words "today you will be with me in paradise" (Lk 23:43) is obvious. Thus heavenly paradise hints at the eternal kingship of Christ, the timelessness of the incarnate Word, and if emphasis were needed S. Anthony writes "Any faithful person is called a 'ruler', after the King of kings of all creation, the Lord Jesus Christ, who rules angels in heaven and men on earth" (Spilsbury III p95).

It is perhaps no surprise that tradition associates a miracle with Anthony's preaching on Jesus of Nazareth, King of the Jews. Whilst Anthony was preaching to a Franciscan gathering, possibly a provincial chapter, in Arles in 1224, S. Francis appeared to one of his hearers (Friar Monaldo) in the form of a cross, and "all those who were present experienced in their hearts a powerful consolation of the Holy Spirit" (Gamboso p102). Francis confirmed the veracity of Anthony's preaching especially that part which referred to the cross of Christ.

Anthony gives Christ a number of kingly titles: re*x noster*, *rex noster Christus, princeps trium ordinum in ecclesia* (a prince of all three orders in the church) and re*x dilecti virtutum* (king of the beloved of all virtues). But he also emphasises that not only is Christ king of all creation and king of all nations, but he is king of every individual soul too. "Jesus Christ, the power and the wisdom of God, made himself a throne to rest upon. This throne is the soul of any just person" (Spilsbury II p122). Here we have a clear Christological teaching, that not only is Christ an all-powerful and infinite king in his divinity, so also is he a king of the soul, a friend of each person in his humanity. If Anthony emphasises the divinity of Christ when he discusses his kingship; so he emphasises Christ's humanity when he discusses his sacred heart.

In a sermon for Easter he asks, why does Christ show the apostles the wounds of the crucifixion? "It seems to me there are four reasons why the Lord showed the Apostles his hands, side and feet. First to show that he had truly risen, and to take away from us all doubtfulness. Second, so that the dove (the Church or the faithful soul) might build her nest in his wounds, as in the clefts of the rock, and hide from the eyes of the hawk that schemes to catch her. Third, to print the signs of his passion as seals upon our hearts. Fourth to ask us to share his sufferings and never again to crucify him with the nails of sin" (Spilsbury I p261).

Following this Easter appearance in the gospel narrative, Anthony reflects on Christ our peace. "Jesus came and stood in the middle of them. 'Peace be with you' he said" (Jn 20:19). Peace is the particular gift of the risen Christ, and it is threefold in its nature: internal, external and eternal. External peace is a gift to the Church and allows us to live with one another. Internal peace is peace of the soul, achieved by divine grace through forgiveness of sin. Eternal peace is peace with God himself, restored to its full dignity by the passion, death and resurrection of Christ.

Anthony reflects that Jesus was in their midst when he gave this gift and he notes that Jesus always occupies a place in the centre, "In heaven, in the Virgin's womb, in the animals' crib, on the gibbet of the cross" (Spilsbury I p258). This centrality should be reflected in our attitude to Christ – he should be central in our lives, so that we on the periphery as it were, may be irradiated by his grace. Anthony also notes (as a concordance) that we read in the Acts of the Apostles, that Peter in imitation of his master "stood up in the centre of his brothers" (Acts 1:15) and he goes on to teach that "when we rise from sin, we should stand in the midst of the brethren; because the midst is charity, which extends to friend and foe alike" (Spilsbury I p260). In other words having received the gift of Christ's peace we should in turn extend peace to others.

Here the emphasis is that we should love Christ because of what he has already done for us. Christ in his humanity has loved us and given himself for us – supremely in his passion and death and all he asks from us is a loving response. But to repeat these 'doings' are doings of Jesus the man, they are not primarily the 'doings' of an infinite Godhead, they are the actions of one who became like us in all things save sin. Of course, this notion is not primarily Anthony's, it is found in holy scripture, particularly the theology of S. John: "We are to love then because he loved us first" (I Jn 4:19).

Also we have a powerful image that Christ is our protector; following the passion and resurrection we can hide from danger in his wounds. This has a clear parallel with a baby or small child hiding in his mother's arms, cowering when afraid ([A little child] "when he is hurt, he runs to his mother's arms" (Spilsbury IV p12)). But this is a human image, Christ is almost our mother and the mother not only cuddles her child, but cares for him with an unlimited love. This image of Christ is a very human image – all too human, for it hints at the vulnerability of Christ and this is underlined by Anthony in his injunction that we do not crucify him again with our sin.

Another particular characteristic of humans is that we have, or are given, names and Anthony is particularly devoted to the name of Jesus. We have already noted in 2.1 that Anthony draws a teaching on the incarnation out of the Holy Name, but he also reflects on the name of Jesus in the context of "your name is an oil poured out" (Sg 1:2). S. Bernard (1090-1153), whom Anthony follows closely here and whom he quotes some thirty-five times, explains three properties of this oil, but Anthony develops the thought further "In the same way the name of Jesus is above every other name of men or angels, for in the name of Jesus every race bows the knee [c.f.Phil 2:10]. If you preach it, you soften hard hearts; if you call upon it, it sooths rough temptations; if you think on it, it enlightens the heart; if you read it, it satisfies the mind" (Spilsbury IV p65/6).

Anthony, not unusually, concludes his theological ruminations with a prayer.

"Name of sweetness, name of salvation. What else is 'Jesus' bur Saviour? Therefore kind Jesus, for your own name's sake, be 'Jesus' to us, so that you who have given the beginning of sweetness, faith may give hope and charity. So, living and dying in them, we may be found fit to come to you; grant this by the prayers of your mother, you who are blessed for ever and ever, Amen" (Spilsbury IV p122).

This emphasis on the humanity of Christ, or more precisely a devotion to Christ's humanity is a distinctive contribution to Christological development. The early doctors and fathers of the church were busy defending the divinity of Christ and his hypostatic union with the eternal Word. The Benedictines and later Cistercians exalted in the triumphant Christ, '*Christus heri, Chritus hodie et in saecula*' but it was the Franciscans who became devoted in a special way to the incarnate person of Jesus (c.f.Huber p27).

Partly this was due to a change of theological emphasis, but it was also, I think, in part due to Anthony's ability to express theological dogma through accessible concepts and language. For Anthony the dialogue in John 14 is central – and he remains close to the biblical text when he writes "It as though of two things exactly alike one might say, if you have seen one you have seen the other" (Spilsbury IV p210). Crucially, God who was largely invisible in the Old Testament and "whose home is in inaccessible light" (1 Tim 6:16) has now been touched and seen. With wonderful economy, Anthony says "You have known him already by knowing me, and have seen him…when you saw me" (ibid).

For Anthony however, the incarnation is not a sudden 'surprise' or a shocking new (divine) departure from the norm, for in creating humans in his own image God had already begun a relationship with them. In the incarnation the relationship between God and man, built up in the old testament is taken to a new level. God enters his own creation. This new level is understood by the church in its Christmas liturgy as a divine exchange, an 'admirable commercium' whereby God who takes on our humanity, draws us humans into his divinity. Christ has truly come to our aid by giving us the gift of his divinity and assuming our humanity, so that we who had been excluded could now be taken into the kingdom of God. He left heaven so that we might gain entrance there and Anthony says "The key is the cross of Christ which opens for us the gate of heaven" (Spilsbury IV p12).

Finally Anthony makes the important point that the Incarnation did not cease at the ascension. Christ did not lay his body aside when he had no further need of it, but rather, at the ascension he took his humanity into the centre of the Godhead. A Christian spirituality centred on Christ, and lived in imitation of him, is a spirituality based on a confidence that our human bodies will be made copies of his glorious body and will come to share in the fullness of divine life itself.

I think it is important to realise that this so called Franciscan school of love, which emphasised that Christ is man's friend, the loving and faithful one who deserves our love in return, was not suddenly invented one day by Francis or Anthony but was something that developed over time, and infused the fledgling order. Of course, Francis as founding father had a profound influence, but he was not a big writer and teacher and his influence was charismatic and largely by word of mouth. Anthony on the other hand, was the order's first theologian, a teacher and a writer, and his influence provided a firm base to complement Francis' charism. I do not see Anthony's Christological approach as derivative of his Franciscan profession, I see Francis and

Anthony independently, but side by side, developing a new way of thinking, a new way of regarding Christ which was both inspired by God and conditioned by the historical influences and demands of the time.

2.3   Mariology

S. Anthony was born in the shadow of Lisbon Cathedral in which he was later baptised. This cathedral is dedicated to Our Lady, and so it is more than likely Anthony would have been particularly aware of Marian celebrations and devotions from an earliest age. Legend tells us that in his teens, Anthony committed himself to the special protection of the Virgin and was particularly devoted to her. Tradition also tells us that on his deathbed in Arcella, north of Padua, he sang, with his brother friars, his favourite hymn in honour of the Blessed Virgin: *O Gloriosa Domina.*

It is very likely then that Anthony had a special personal devotion to Our Lady, but what of his more formal theological stance; what did S. Anthony teach about the Blessed Virgin Mary? There are many, many Marian references throughout Anthony's sermons, and additionally he wrote four specific Marian sermons as part of his cycle for solemnities and feasts. The four are for the feasts of the Nativity, the Annunciation, the Purification and the Assumption of Our Lady, and it is in these that we find the core of Anthony's Marian theology.

The Birth of the Blessed Virgin Mary celebrated on 8 September, is now kept as the feast of the Immaculate Conception of the Blessed Virgin Mary following the papal bull *Ineffabilis Deus* of 8 September 1854. The doctrine of the Immaculate Conception as such, was not new, and had been widely believed for many centuries, but following the pronouncement of Pope Pius IX it is a matter of faith which every catholic is bound to believe. The precise doctrine is that "the Blessed Virgin Mary, in the first instant of her conception, was, by a unique grace and privilege of Almighty God in view of the merits of Jesus Christ, the Saviour of the human race, preserved exempt from all stain of original sin." The stain of original sin was not removed, but excluded from her soul. Was this the teaching of the Evangelical Doctor?

Firstly, we must realise that doctrine takes time to be understood, formulated and defined. Butler tells us that "the adoption of the feast in the cathedral of Lyons about the year 1140 was the occasion of a protest by S. Bernard of Clairvaux which precipitated a theological controversy lasting three hundred years" (Butler, September p73). S. Thomas Aquinas opposed the feast as did the Dominicans but the Order of Friars Minor adopted it in 1263. S Anthony then lived in the midst of a time of discussion and debate concerning the nature and status of the Virgin Mary. What precisely did S. Anthony believe?

Following Augustine, Anthony declared that Mary was full of grace, filled by God before all others. He describes her as an untouched cedar and as a full moon, resplendent in glory without the spots of a waxing or waning moon. She was absolutely free of concupiscence and perfect in every way, but Anthony also states that Mary "was sanctified in her mother's womb and guarded by angels" (Spilsbury III p394). In her life she never committed the sin of pride and was unparalleled in her perfection.

As far as the modern expression of the doctrine is concerned, the key question here is when did the sanctification of which Anthony speaks take place? Was it at the very moment of her conception or sometime in her mother's womb before her birth, that is was she preserved from the outset from original sin or was that stain *removed* from her soul? Anthony is not explicit, and therefore cannot be said to teach the doctrine of the Immaculate Conception in all its fullness, but equally we cannot be certain what Anthony might have said if it were possible for us to ask him.

Anthony quotes Augustine saying "I make an exception of the Virgin Mary. When discussing sin, I do not wish (for the Lord's own honour) to raise any question whatsoever about her. Greater grace was given to her, to overcome every kind of sin, than simply to conceive and bear him, who, as all agree, had no sin (Spilsbury I p173). Huber is clear that Anthony taught and countered those who attacked the church, and asserts that "Anthony seems to have prepared the way for his illustrious confrere, the venerable Duns Scotus and the latter's teacher William of Ware, in their defence of the doctrine of the Immaculate Conception of the Blessed Virgin Mary" (Huber p79).

Anthony, following S. Augustine again, is clear that Mary does not have her merits by right, but on account of her Son. Alluding to the Magnificat he urges "Look upon the rainbow; that is, consider the beauty, holiness and dignity of blessed Mary; and bless with heart and mouth and deed her Son who made her thus (Spilsbury III p400). Mary's holiness derives from that most intimate of relationships between a mother and a child, Mary's divine motherhood caused her to be exalted above all human kind. "Blessed then is the womb of the glorious virgin, who for nine months was worthy to bear all good, the supreme good, the blessedness of the angels and the reconciliation of sinners" (Spilsbury I p173).

In conclusion, it seems Anthony did not express the doctrine of the Immaculate Conception in its modern (explicit) formulation, but that he believed and taught something extremely close, which paved the way for later formalisations. We can, I think, be confident in a retrospective sense, that if confronted with the modern declaration, S. Anthony would have had no theological qualms with it.

Having considered the nature of the birth of Mary it is natural to the modern mind to consider the nature of her death, although for Anthony this constitutes an anagogical interpretation of scripture, pointing towards heavenly bliss. The extent to which one considers Mary's death in some sense as a universal pattern or as a singular event might colour one's approach. Here I will follow what seems appropriate to the modern mind, and consider the nature of Mary's death as a question of doctrine.

We have no biblical or other records of the exact nature of Mary's death, but it is a theological issue because of a general belief that death occurs on account of human corruption and sin. If Mary was sinless, then she could not have died – at least not in the normal sense. By the fifth and sixth centuries there were two schools of thought: firstly that at her human death, Mary was borne body and soul directly into heaven. The second school thought that at her death, Mary's soul was borne into heaven and her body was transported incorrupt, into storage by Angels to await the general resurrection at the end of earthly time.

By mediaeval times, the bodily assumption of Mary body and soul into heaven was widely believed and was defended by SS. Albert the Great, Thomas Aquinas and Bonaventure, but there was also scholars who regarded the doctrine of the assumption with varying degrees of scepticism. Protestant Christians of the Reformation largely rejected the doctrine of the assumption, but Catholics had their belief confirmed by the papal bull *Munificentissimus Deus*, promulgated on 1 November 1950 by Pope Pius XII. It is an article of the Catholic faith that "at the end of her earthly life, the immaculate mother of God, Mary ever virgin, was taken up body and soul into the glory of heaven."

The questions for us are how does S. Anthony of Padua fit into this (necessarily brief) historical picture, and how did he express this doctrine? As I have said for S. Anthony the doctrine is revealed through an anagogical interpretation of scripture. Anthony sees Esther as a type prefiguring Mary. Esther prefigures Mary in several ways, but in particular as Esther is crowned queen by Assuerus who loved her more than any other woman, so Mary is crowned Queen of Heaven by Christ (c.f. Esther 2:15-17).

Returning to the theme of exchange which we have already mentioned, Anthony writes "Because blessed Mary crowned the Son of God with the diadem of flesh on the day of his espousals, the day of his conception, when the divine nature was united to human nature, like a bridegroom to a bride, in the bride chamber of that same. Virgin: therefore this same Son has crowned his mother today with the crown of heavenly glory" (Spilsbury III p435). And Anthony goes on to say that once crowned Mary occupies a heavenly throne above all the angels and saints, immediately next to Christ himself.

In another place Anthony quotes the second antiphon at Lauds for the feast of the assumption, saying Mary was taken up (*assumpta est*) to the heavenly courts where the King of Kings sits upon a starry throne (c.f. Spilsbury III p434) and in another concordance paraphrasing the song of songs he exclaims "Go forth then! See the mother of Solomon wearing the crown wherewith her Son crowned her on the day of her Assumption!" (Spilsbury III p435). Huber asserts that Anthony "defended the corporal Assumption of the Blessed Virgin Mary as hardly any other father of the Church had done before his time" (Huber p79). He goes on to add that Anthony's real theological contribution was to recognise the assumption as a consequence of Mary's divine motherhood. As the Immaculate Conception was the 'preparation' for Mary's maternity, so the assumption was the inevitable 'consequence' of it. Huber even suggests that it was this theological link between Mary's divine motherhood (*ex qua carnem accepit*) and the assumption, which was first recognised or taught by Anthony, that, in part, paved the way for the Church's formal declaration of the doctrine of the assumption (c.f. Huber p80 & p83 n22).

To what extent S. Anthony 'paved the way' it is hard to judge, and as we have seen he was not unique in his teaching, but Pope Pius XI does refer explicitly to S. Anthony saying "Among the holy writers who at that time employed statements and various images and analogies of sacred scripture to illustrate and to confirm the doctrine of the Assumption, which was piously believed; the Evangelical Doctor, St. Anthony of Padua, holds a special place" (*Munificentissimus Deus* 29). As Anthony was earlier than Bonaventure, Albert, Aquinas and others, to whom the document also refers, we can legitimately claim some influence and status for Anthony, even if (as in the doctrine of the Immaculate Conception) Anthony's formulation does not encompass the fullness of the modern formulation.

Finally a legend taken from *Stellarium Coronae Gloriossimae Virgins* written by Pelbarto of Timisoara, Venice in 1586, tells us that Anthony was an apostle of the Assumption on account of a heavenly vision. "On the vigil of this Marian feast which even then was celebrated on the 15 August, Anthony refused to go down to common prayer with his confreres. He did not want to hear the words in the reading of the Martyrology and a homily of S. Jerome that disturbed his faith. These words are 'The tomb of the Blessed Virgin is still empty today. Some doubt whether that most holy body was raised from the dead, participating in some way in the glorious immortality of Christ her Son and they go about saying that it was taken and placed elsewhere.'

The Saint therefore remained alone to pray in his cell. After a short while an angel appeared and asked him 'Why, brother, did you not go down to community prayer?' He answered that he did not feel like listening to those words filled with doubt. Immediately the Madonna appeared surrounded by a blinding light and accompanied by a choir of angels. She assured him of the great privileges that had been granted her, encouraging him to be courageous in preaching it to all with full assurance" (Gamboso p103).

Of course Anthony sees Mary prefigured in the Old Testament and develops many beautiful metaphors and similes to convey his theology. To consider just a few, he likens Mary (as we have seen) to a full moon, which has no spots like a waxing or waning moon. He sees her as the ark of the covenant, the tabernacle in which Christ, the new law, the Son of Justice is housed. He sees her as a sheep, who gave her pure white wool to clothe the son of God, and he sees her as an olive tree, luxuriant and thick with fruit, signifying peace and mercy, or "[Mary] like a cypress raised herself on high above the height of all the angels"(Spilsbury III p436). At other times Mary is a garden in which Christ is planted and from which he receives his human nature.

Anthony also refers to Mary as a rock in the desert which is untouched by man, or more dramatically, a place where no seed may be planted. He refers to her as the burning bush which is not consumed and as a lily which does not lose its blossom when it emits its fragrance. In these metaphors Anthony teaches that Mary remained ever a virgin. "So the blessed Virgin did not lose the flower of virginity when she gave birth to the Saviour" (Spilsbury III p406).

Finally, Anthony refers to Mary as a rainbow. As a rainbow appears as the sun enters a cloud, so when the new law, the Son of Justice enters the virgin's womb she is as a rainbow. She is a sign of peace and reconciliation a "sign of the covenant ....between God and sinners" (Spilsbury III p399). Here Anthony seems to be teaching the doctrine of Mary as the mediatrix of all graces, and again this is a title which would be later be ascribed to Mary by Pope Pius X and confirmed by Pope Pius XI.

So much then for these doctrinal teachings. Anthony also sees Mary as the supreme example or pattern of how to live a human life, and develops a moral teaching from a consideration of her verbal utterances in the gospels. S. Anthony observes that in the Gospels of Luke and John there are six utterances of Mary, each of which corresponds to one of her virtues and which can lead or direct us in a virtuous life. If we consider these in turn, Mary's first utterance is to the Angel of the Annunciation and she asks "but how can this come about?" (Lk 1:34). Anthony says this shows Mary's inviolable virginity: her particular chastity and the purity of her way of life in general.

Mary's second utterance; "I am the handmaid of the Lord" (Lk 1:38) demonstrates Mary's obedience and humility. Her declaration of the Magnificat "My soul proclaims the greatness of the Lord" (Lk 1:46) demonstrates her thanks and exultation for the blessings given to her. Mary's fourth utterance "My child why have you done this to us" (Lk 2:48) shows Mary solicitude, or her consideration and concern for Christ.

In S. John's gospel Mary's fifth utterance is "they have no wine" (Jn 2:3) which Anthony says shows Mary's compassion and following this the sixth and final utterance "do whatever he tells you" (Jn 2:5) demonstrates Mary's absolute trust in Christ's power. At many other times when Mary might have been expected to speak, e.g. at the passion, no words are recorded by the evangelists and we can think of Mary pondering all things in her heart.

Anthony further compares these six utterances to the six steps that led to Solomon's throne, the six leaves of the lily and the six branches of the candlestick. Whilst all these numerical similarities may sound quaint if not contrived to the modern ear we must remember again that the mediaeval friars had few books, they preached without notes and many of these constructions act as *aides memoires*. Having said that we must not dismiss Anthony's teaching too quickly, for his purpose is to teach a virtuous way of life, and to encourage his hearers to chastity, humility, thankfulness, trust etc. In addition to identifying Mary's virtues he also describes her as the morning star or the star of the sea. Mary is the guide to her Son, she puts darkness to flight and she directs us through the world to the safety of heaven.

Finally, we might consider some of Anthony's addresses and prayers to the Virgin Mary, which are both numerous and beautiful. As is often the case Anthony ends his sermons with a prayer but all four Marian sermons have prayers in them and at their conclusion. Considering some of the terms of address Anthony uses, on imagining Mary being led to the throne room of heaven, in his sermon for the assumption, he exclaims, almost ecstatically: "O immeasurable dignity of Mary! O inexpressible sublimity of grace! O unsearchable depth of mercy!" (Spilsbury III p434). (*"O inestimabilis Mariae dignitas; O inennaribilis gratiae sublimitas, O investigabilis misericordiae profunditas."*) What affection and what love for Mary are expressed in these words.

Most of Anthony's prayers to the Virgin ask that she may share some of her grace with us so that we may be lead from sin, through forgiveness to the fullness of divine life. On the feast of the purification of Our Lady he prays:

"We ask you, then, our Lady, and chosen mother of God,
To purify us from the blood of sin,
to make us bear the burning fire of contrition,
in the wax of confession and the tow of satisfaction:
so that we may be made fit to attain the light and glory of the
	heavenly Jerusalem.
May he grant this whom you offered today in the temple and
	to whom be glory and honour for evermore. Amen."

(Spilsbury III p427).

Again at the end of his sermon for the Assumption he prays:

"We ask you then, our Lady, great Mother of God, lifted high above the choirs of angels, to fill the cup of our heart with heavenly grace; to make it gleam with the gold of wisdom; to make it solid with the power of your virtue; to adorn it with the precious stones of virtues; to pour upon us, O blessed olive tree, the oil of your mercy to cover the multitude if our sins. By you may we be found fit to be raised to the height of heavenly glory, and to be blessed with the blessed, by the power of Jesus Christ your Son, who this day has raised you above the choirs of angels, crowned you with the diadem of his kingdom, and set you upon the throne of eternal light. To him be honour and glory, through endless ages. Let the whole Church say: Amen Alleluia." (Spilsbury III p427).

In his favourite hymn sung on his deathbed, Anthony calls Mary his glorious queen, and addresses her as the one who has become the window of heaven (*caeli fenestra facta es*). He addresses her as mother of grace and prays that she will protect him and take him to herself in his hour of death (*Tu nos ab hoste protege, et hora mortis suscipe*).

To conclude: Anthony not only showed great devotion to the Blessed Virgin Mary and no doubt taught by his example, but he also was ahead of his time in preaching and teaching about the theological role of Mary. From her divine motherhood, he explained her Immaculate Conception and Glorious Assumption. He recognised her as ever virgin and he did much to lay the foundations for future Mariology and formal ecclesial pronouncements.

2.4   Ecclesiology and the Theology of the Religious Life

When we think of the mediaeval Church, the huge numbers of Christians who were still unable to read or write, and the proliferation of heresies of different kinds we can grasp something of the enormous task facing the new orders of S. Francis and S. Dominic. In mediaeval times the absolute priority was the huge task of preaching and teaching orthodox Christianity across Europe and the world. There was not at this time any call or need for reflection on the nature of the church itself because other needs were far more pressing.

To put the same point another way the Dogmatic Constitution on the Church, *Lumen Gentium*, one of the key documents produced by the Second Vatican Council in November 1964 is an essentially *modern* document. Not modern on account of its dating, but modern in the sense that the church had come of age. A certain time had arrived when it was appropriate for the church to consider or reconsider herself, to adopt a reflexive stance, to try in some way to formulate a mystery, in order to progress and evolve.

S. Anthony of Padua's reflections on the church, then, whilst not unique, embody something of a modern stance, since they look beyond the immediate task in hand for the thirteenth century friar, and they demonstrate a depth of thought and a perspicacity which, whilst perhaps not so deeply profound or as wonderfully uplifting as Anthony's teachings on Mary, are both relevant and timely for the modern mind and the modern church.

One of Anthony's favourite themes is Noah's ark which prefigures the establishment of the church. In his sermon for Sexagesima he likens the smooth wood of which the ark was built to those saints who are holy and perfect and who make up the church; and as we have already noted, he likens the pitch with which the wood was covered to the love and mercy of the saints on the inside, and the good works of the saints on the outside. But Anthony goes further than this and sees the dimensions of the ark as significant. He says the three hundred cubits which are the length of the ark tell us of the three categories of people who make up the church: prelates, religious and married people. The width of the ark which is fifty cubits reminds us of the penitents of the church, because it was fifty days after Easter that the Holy Spirit was poured out on the Apostles and the fiftieth psalm is the *Miserere me* (Have mercy upon me) in which forgiveness is promised to the penitent. Finally the height of the ark, thirty cubits, reminds us of the ordinary faithful who believe in the trinity. Fanciful though this may seem, we must remember again that it is something of an *aide memoir*, and the key teaching at the end of this section is "Christ goes out from the bosom of the Father…..to build his church, in which the incorruptible and everlasting harvest is to be stored" (Spilsbury I p38.).

The following week, as it were, in his sermon for Quinquagesima, Anthony describes the church as the mystical body of Christ, and he says that as Christ was scourged by Pilate so the church is scourged by sinful men, who crucify Christ over and over. Anthony writes, "Alas, alas, once more the entire mystical body of Christ, the church is crucified and killed!" (Spilsbury I p66). There is a clear Augustinian theme here, deriving ultimately from S. Paul, that the members of the church are one body with Christ at the head.

The concept of oneness or unity found in Augustine is important to Anthony too. A little later (Pentecost XIV) he says that Christ's tunic which "was seamless, woven in one piece from neck to hem" (Jn 19:23) symbolises the unity of the Church which sinners and false Christians wish to tear apart. Anthony was a tireless defender of the unity of the church and this gives us an important insight into his reasons for countering the teachings of heretics. For Anthony, countering heresy was not solely an academic matter or a question of doctrine, but countering heresy was a fundamental ecclesiological task, that they might all be one as we are one (c.f. Jn 17:20). For Anthony it was impossible to be a Christian outside the unity of the church.

Anthony is also clear that membership of the church, which derives from a unity with Jesus Christ the head, is only established through baptism. Nobody enters the church unless he is baptised and united to the body of Christ. Those who are called by a preacher may come to receive this gift by which they will unite themselves to the members of the church and be able to share in all the spiritual goods of the Father's house. Here Anthony teaches that the church is not only a human community but also a supernatural community, a means of grace and a pathway to a heavenly home. Jerusalem, when understood anagogically, refers to this heavenly home, the church triumphant, when those called by Christ will be truly citizens of heaven.

Anthony's reflections on the church also have a marked Petrine theme, and he refers to the church as the barque of Peter. Anthony notes that Jesus got into one of the boats – the one belonging to Peter (Lk 5:3) – from which he taught the crowds. Anthony says "The ship is the church of Jesus Christ, committed to Peter's care" (Spilsbury II p117). Anthony goes on to reflect that the church needs a competent guide, a skilled helmsman, a leader "to keep it safe among dangers" (ibid) but he also observes that Peter was an illiterate and ignorant man, "an uneducated layman" (Acts 4:13).

For Anthony the transformation came about through Peter being the first to recognise and declare Christ's divinity. In the Lord's response to Peter, Jesus says "I say not that you will be called, but that you are Peter, from me the rock" (Spilsbury IV p135). Peter is not called a rock, but he truly is a rock. Peter was made a rock by Christ. Peter becomes a part of the foundation of the church which is Christ, for as S. Paul says "For the foundation nobody can lay any other than the one which has already been laid, that is Jesus Christ" (I Cor 3:11).

Having been made a part of the foundation of the church by Christ himself, we can understand better Christ entrusting to Peter the keys of the kingdom of heaven. Anthony says Peter was "set at the head of the apostles and of the church…he who confessed before the rest, is given the keys before the rest" (Spilsbury IV p137).

There are three important teachings to be developed here. Firstly the teaching of Petrine primacy is obvious: Peter is both head of the apostles and head of the church, and as such enjoys the power and jurisdiction of the keys. The second more subtle teaching (here Anthony quotes S. Jerome) is that the other apostles share in this power and judicial authority because Jesus gave the gift of the Holy Spirit to *them all* after his resurrection (Jn 20:22), but that they can only exercise it *with* Peter.

In a modern context, the teaching is that whereas all bishops enjoy authority over their priests, and all bishops and priests can absolve sins, they can only do this on account of their communion with Peter – that is their communion with Rome. Although "the whole church has this power in its priests and bishops; yet Peter received it in a special way, so that all might understand that whoever should separate themselves from the unity of faith and his company, can neither be absolved from sin nor enter heaven" (Spilsbury IV p137).

The third teaching is that on account of Peter's transformation by Christ, he is no longer an uneducated layman, but on account of his position he is most wise (*sedens in cathedra sapientissimus*). According to Anthony, Peter was most wise, because of the time he had spent with Jesus, and had thereby been schooled not in the wisdom of the world but in the wisdom of heaven (c.f. Huber p44). Further it was for Peter in particular that Christ prayed that his faith might not fail (Lk 22:32), and so Peter was transformed by Christ from an idiot into a savant.

Again Anthony's presentation or formulation is not in the modern idiom, but Huber sees Anthony's teaching as meaning "only one thing: papal infallibility" (Huber p44). In other words, that Peter and his successors when speaking ex-cathedra on matters of faith and morals cannot err. We must observe that Anthony is not mentioned in Vatican I's dogmatic constitution on the church: *Pastor Aeternus*, in which the doctrine of papal infallibility was formally defined, and his influence cannot be directly traced, but we can be sure of Anthony's early recognition of the pre-eminence of S. Peter and again we can be confident, I think, that presented with the modern formulation of the doctrine, Anthony would have been in complete agreement. Anthony concludes his sermon for Pentecost V with the following prayer:

"Dearest brothers, let us pray the Lord Jesus Christ himself
To make us go up into Simon's ship by obedience,
To sit in the ivory throne of humility and chastity,
To steer our ship away from earthly things towards the deeps
   of contemplation,
And to let down our nets for a catch; so that with a multitude
   of good works we may attain to him, who is the good and
   supreme God.
May he be pleased to grant this, who lives and reigns for ever
   and ever.
Amen"

(Spilsbury II p128).

Having considered something of S. Anthony's ecclesiology, it is fitting here to consider his teaching on the religious life. The first indication we get about this is that when Canon Fernando left his Augustinian brothers he took the name Anthony, after the little Franciscan house at S. Anthony de Olivais near Coimbra, and indirectly after S. Anthony of Egypt. Anthony of Egypt (c. 251 – 356), left the world to live in a cave in the desert where he was eventually joined by others seeking God. He is often considered to be the father of western monasticism, and this monasticism was essentially a life of prayer and contemplation. By choosing this name, I think it is reasonable to infer, the Lisbon canon indicates something of his own conception of the religious life.

Furthermore biographical sources attest to Anthony's frequent and lengthy periods of solitary prayer. After the disastrous trip to Morocco Anthony was eventually sent to Montepaulo in the hills of Romagna, where a grotto was built for him, in which he spent long hours in prayer. "After fulfilling the morning community prayers, [he] would daily retire to the cell, taking with himself some bread and a small container of water. In this way he spent the day alone forcing the body to serve the spirit" (Assidua 7:8). Later in life he retired to Camposampiero, north of Padua, where it is said he had a house built for him in a tree in which he could retire to pray.

Anthony was then a contemplative, a man of prayer, and whilst he no doubt valued preaching and teaching, and the common life of the brothers, he understood that these other activities were dependent on a life of contemplation. His prayerful relationship with God animated everything else he did.

If we consider Anthony's writings, his sermons to religious are invariably about contemplation. The contemplative must be dead to the world, and leave behind the chaff of temporal things, being as one buried in the tomb (c.f. Spilsbury I p238). "He must gaze on him to whom he offers the sacrifice of his prayer" (ibid. p244). Again the contemplative should be with Mary and John at the foot of the cross. "Let us lift up our eyes then, and let us look on Jesus the author of our salvation. Let us consider our Lord hanging on the cross fixed with nails" (Spilsbury IV p225). And again using the idea of a ladder (the ladder in Jacob's dream) to climb to God, the sixth rung is "the contemplation of heavenly glory" (Spilsbury I p128).

Contemplation is not an intellectual process, it is not meditation or thinking about God, nor addressing him in supplication, but is an awareness of being in his presence. It is as the beloved in the presence of his lover, it is adoration. This is not possible says Anthony, by human effort alone, but contemplation is a gift of grace. "Contemplation is not from the will of the contemplative but the disposition of the creator" (Spilsbury II p407). Contemplation is recognition of an utter dependence on God, and is a means by which the contemplative penetrates heaven itself.

For Anthony then, contemplation was at the heart of religious life, but as contemplation is a gift, how does one prepare for it, how does one make oneself ready? The answer for Anthony is by silence and prayer. Silence obviously entails freedom from noise and physical distraction. "You cannot see your face if you look into troubled and moving waters. If you want to see Christ's face appear in you when you look, sit down and be quiet" (Spilsbury IV p248). And again "The tongue should be controlled and whoever does not silence it proves he is without real religion" (Spilsbury I p382). But more than this, silence is an interior silence, a flight from distraction. When we pray we should be one with God, undivided, and as Anthony says: "A divided mind does not pray, so they should labour to be whole, that their tongues accord with their hearts" (Spilsbury II p262).

And of prayer Anthony says it should be constant, but that there are three kinds, "mental, vocal and manual" (Spilsbury I p397), which express a person's love of God. He quotes the psalmist "Hear my voice O Lord (of heart and mouth and work) with which I have cried to thee. My heart hath said to thee I have sought thy face" (ibid). All prayer is about seeking God, that we might recognise his nature in order to become more like Him. When we go to pray we should go to our rooms and close the door. That is we should enter the secret chamber of the heart and close the door of the senses. (c.f. Spilsbury I p96). But note, prayer does not exclude good works, the sense in which prayer may be manual, for Anthony says "He ceases not to pray who ceases not to do good" (Spilsbury I p397).

Considering vocal prayer, Anthony says Jesus spoke in no uncertain terms about the importance of prayer: "Ask and you shall receive" (Lk 11:9), but Anthony expands this considering the question of what we might or should ask for. He notes that "the Lord rebukes those who ask for temporal things" (Spilsbury I p367) and says when we recognise that God is our Father and we are his children, everything that exists is nothing compared to God's love. So we should ask for the love of God, and since God is love, the gift of love is the gift of God himself. "If we ask for love, then the Father himself, who is love, will give us what he himself is, namely love" (Spilsbury I p364).

To summarise he says "prayer is the disposition of the man who holds to God; and is a certain familiarity and loving conversation with him" (Spilsbury I p368) for those whose life is centred on prayer will be centred not on the world but on heaven where their treasure is, and hence that is where our hearts should be also.

In addition to the life of contemplation and prayer Anthony teaches that the religious should develop the virtues of humility and obedience. He speaks often of humility, and to abbreviate his treatment somewhat, he says humility is the most important of the virtues. Humility is a recognition of one's own state before God and is a precondition for the exercise of the other virtues, living in submission to the Divine will. Of course, Anthony points out that in Jesus Christ we have a perfect model of humility. He quotes the well known passage to the Philippians (2:7-8) and commenting upon "He then went down with them and came to Nazareth and lived under their authority" (Lk 2:51) he emphasises the 'went down' which shows Jesus' humility, and indicates that we too should "come down, sit in the dust.........because the Son of God went down" (Spilsbury III p 337) rather than following our tendency to inflate ourselves, and exaggerate our own importance.

Interpreting "Every good tree brings forth good fruit and an evil tree brings forth evil fruit" (Matt 7:17), Anthony understand this morally, that a good tree is a symbol of a righteous person, who has the "root of humility, the trunk of obedience, the branches of charity, the leaves of holy preaching and sweet fruit of heavenly contemplation" (Spilsbury II p191). The quality and depth of the roots influence the health of the rest of the tree and Anthony says, "true humility abases itself, the more deeply it is rooted, and so it is raised up the higher" (ibid). He who is truly humble shares in the absolute humility of Christ who was obedient unto death on the cross, and may thereby hope to share in the exultation of the resurrection.

In his sermon for Pentecost XI, Anthony prays: "Let us, then, dearest brothers, ask the Lord Jesus Christ himself to take away from us the boasting of the Pharisee, and to imprint upon our hearts the Gospel of his humility; that we may go up to the temple of his glory and, set at his right hand in the general resurrection, may deserve to rejoice with him. May he grant this, who died and rose again, to whom be honour and glory for ever and ever. Amen" (Spilsbury II p277).

We have seen here that Anthony's righteous person has the trunk of obedience. If humility is the root of all the other virtues, then obedience is their guardian and protector. Obedience or in Latin *obedentia* is really derived from *'obaudentia',* and *audio*, to listen or hear. Obedience then is the virtue of 'hearing' or submitting to legitimate authority. Not following rules as such, but an inclination to compliance. 'Thy will be done' as we pray daily in the Our Father.

Again in Jesus Christ we have a perfect model of obedience, and the model teaches us that we should be obedient not out of fear of retribution but out of love. Obedience is not blind submission or slavish subservience, but proceeds from love, and Anthony teaches that this is what Jesus meant when he said "If you keep my commandments you will remain in my love" (Jn 15:10). Jesus kept the Father's commandments and was one in love with him, and similarly our obedience ensures we remain one in love with Jesus himself.

I want to conclude by considering a more practical, or to put it another way a less theological aspect of Anthony's teaching on the religious life. In 1220 Cardinal Ugolino was persuaded by Francis to be protector of the fledgling Franciscan order, to keep the friars faithful to the rule but also to represent the friars in the heart of church life. In 1227 Ugolino was elected as Pope Gregory IX, and we are told that Anthony, whilst on business in Rome, preached before him and the Roman curia around 1228 and Pope Gregory was so astounded by his fluency and mastery of scripture that he declared him "The Armory of Holy Scripture" (Armarium divinae scripturae (Clasen p85)).

Some years later Anthony was to meet Pope Gregory again. After S. Francis death in 1226 some dissention developed between the brothers about the precise interpretation of the rule. As the Order grew and expanded, and as their needs changed there were those who said the rule needed to be interpreted and revised, whereas those loyal to the memory of Francis said the rule must be obeyed without any amendments or interpretation (*sine glossa*). Was Francis' deathbed testament of the same status as the rule itself? Could the brothers own books for study? Could they establish houses of study and if so, who owned them? What was it legitimate for the friars to do in the face of lax clergy and how, in general, was the growing Order to be administered?

The Franciscan chapter of 1230 "was one of the most unruly on record in the order's brief history" (Robson p149) and threatened to damage the order profoundly. Eventually it was decided to seek a definite ruling on the contentious issues from Pope Gregory IX, and a delegation including Anthony of Padua, who was by now provincial of Upper Italy, was sent to Rome. The meetings led to the papal bull *Quo elongati* of September 1230, which as I have already mentioned ruled that Francis' deathbed testament was not canonically binding on the friars. It also ruled that the friars were unable to own any books or property but that they might have use of them, as directed by the ministers general and provincial. And it ruled that those versed in theology might preach without taking the preaching exam unless the minister general decreed otherwise.

This bull did much to pave the way for the expansion of the fraternity particularly into academic life and the emerging universities; it led it away from the absolute strictness of Francis' vision and it made the little brothers of S. Francis into a mainstream religious order. In the bull, Gregory IX claimed that he was able to make his ruling on account of his long and intimate acquaintanceship with Francis, and his earlier role of assisting in the composition of the rule and obtaining papal recognition of it. It is unclear how much influence the Chapter's delegation had on the papal deliberations. Did they simply inform him of the points of the dispute, or did they also advise him on his future ruling?

The answer to this question must, of necessity, be purely speculative for no historical evidence is readily available, but given that Gregory had already met Anthony, given that he had recognised his wisdom and deep knowledge of the Bible and given that Gregory IX canonised Anthony in near record time, and even faster than S. Francis himself, it would be remarkable if Gregory had not consulted Anthony about *Quo elongati* at all.

For Francis study was a threat to sanctity. Firstly, he thought the scholar is likely to become puffed up with his own learning, and make himself superior to his unlettered brethren. Secondly, scholarship by its very nature requires books, even libraries, it requires paper and pens which were luxuries in the middle ages and it requires some stability and material comfort; wandering beggars are rarely top scholars. Francis thought these things were a threat, or perhaps even entirely antithetical to holy poverty. Finally it seems that Francis was concerned that study might lead his brothers away from prayer and as we have seen in his famous instruction to Anthony, study may be undertaken, so long as the spirit of prayer and devotion are not extinguished.

The genius of Anthony was to show that study and prayer are not enemies. Indeed Anthony knew that many of the saints, especially in the patristic era, had been both skilled theologians and holy prelates. For Anthony, the study of theology and living the life of virtue were opposite sides of the same coin. Firstly and foremost this is because the study of theology was not an end in itself, it was not legitimised by curiosity; it was, and was only, a tool to enable the message of the gospel to be more clearly and persuasively preached.

Secondly a study of the biblical texts was not a literary or linguistic exercise but was directed towards a better understanding of Christian living. The key for Anthony was not human regard, but the regard a man had before God. Man does not set about improving himself by study, but is improved by humility and divine grace. He underlines this when he mentions the prelates, whose "eyes, the light of reason and understanding have grown dim with the love of earthly things.....[who] do not recognise that they have lost

God's grace" (Spilsbury I p289). In other words, not so much scholarship, but a love of earthly things and the failure to recognise dependence on divine grace is what leads away from God.

In Anthony, then, the living of the Christian life, virtue and knowledge of holy scripture are combined. A study of theology lead to a holy life and a holy life enabled and was conducive towards a study of theology. The whole was animated by prayer which was understood as an ongoing and uninterrupted conversation with God.

2.5   *Mystical Theology*

The terms 'mysticism', 'mystic' and 'mystical theology' may be understood in a variety of ways. Our English words derive from the Greek *mystērion* meaning mystery or *mystokos* meaning mystical, which both have their ultimate root in the verb *myein* meaning to close, as in to close one's eyes. The implication of this derivation is that a mystery is somehow closed or secret: mystical truths are not open or available to all.

The prophet Daniel says "there is a God in heaven who reveals mysteries" (Dan 2:28) and the word 'reveals' here, shows the mystery is not ordinarily accessible. Christ tells his disciples "the secret (*mysterion*) of the kingdom of God is given to you" (Mk 4:11) and in the Pauline letters *mysterion* occurs frequently with the connotation that in Christ new mysteries have been revealed and the Christians are the guardians or keepers of those mysteries. For example, Paul says "people must think of us as Christ's servants, stewards entrusted with the mysteries of God" (1 Cor 4:1) and similarly "God made me responsible for delivering God's message to you, the message which was a mystery hidden for generations..........the mystery is Christ among you" (Col 1 26-27).

This notion of mystery is central to Pauline theology and it is no coincidence that we sometimes refer to the Mass as the 'holy mysteries'. As we have noted early biblical exegetes looked for layers of meaning in sacred texts and Origen in particular was aware of a mystical meaning, hidden in the text. A deeper meaning perhaps, that God wanted to keep hidden from the eyes of the profane or uninitiated.

In modern times, particularly since the Second Vatican Council, there has been a move away from contrasting the mystical with the ordinary, a move away from classifying mystical experiences as a set disjoint from all other experiences. Thomas Merton emphasises that there are many ways to experience God, and whilst they are not all qualitatively the same, what they have in common, namely that they are all 'of God' is what is of most importance. "Call it faith, call it (at a more advanced stage) contemplative illumination, call it the sense of God or even mystical union, all these are different aspects and levels of the same kind of realization........ a new awareness of ourselves in Christ" (Merton p175).

Similarly echoing Merton, Bernard McGinn has suggested the essential element of Christian mysticism is union, with Christ or with God "in which the individual personality is lost" (McGinn pxvi). The mystic is so completely aware of the presence of God that he almost becomes one with God, losing his own identity, becoming almost absorbed into the Godhead.

To conclude then, the suggestion that Anthony of Padua was a mystic is to suggest that he was particularly intimate with God. Either that God had revealed himself to Anthony in a special way, or that Anthony through prayer and contemplation had a particularly close union with the Divine. It does not really matter whether we consider that Anthony's mystic experiences were 'secret' in some sense, or whether they were just relatively unusual. The questions for us are: what can we reliably know about them and what may we infer from them?

Before we come to these questions it is also worth mentioning that once armed with a sense of the mystical, or the idea of a mystical experience as a particular close encounter with God, then mystical theology becomes the science of understanding these experiences. The mystic theologian must reflect on mystical experience and try to describe and communicate it, in order to evaluate it and consider its implications. In other word the mystic theologian must attempt to move from the 'raw data' of mystic experience to an understanding of the event in order that judgements, inferences and possible future decisions may be made. With this in mind, we may ask to what extent S. Anthony's writings contain any reflections and inferences which may be understood as deriving, in a special way, from any mystical experiences he himself may have had, and then we may be able to answer the derivative question: was S. Anthony of Padua a mystic theologian?

Let us reconsider for a moment those whom I have described as the principle influences upon S. Anthony. Firstly, S. Augustine – was he a mystic? Most theologians recognise the profound spirituality of Augustine, particularly as it pertains to the notions of Christian development and conversion, but express doubt about Augustine being a mystic. Butler writes "He soon left for Ostia, where he is said to have shared with his mother the 'vision of Ostia' a quasi-mystical experience or a form of sacred enlightenment, already sensed in pre-conversion 'ascents of the mind' at Milan. It is generally agreed that these and other personal religious experiences reported by Augustine cannot be classed as mystical contemplation" (Butler August p281).

I have discussed above how Augustine came to learn from Ambrose that scripture needed interpretation, that it is the spirit of the text that gives life, and Wiseman says that

"Augustine was in fact experiencing the same kind of 'mystical interpretation' of scripture that had been advocated by Origen in the previous century" (Wiseman p101). But this is not particularly mystical in the sense of close union with the Divine as discussed above.

Perhaps Augustine's best claim to be a mystic, derives from his writings in the *Confessions*. There is undoubtedly something remarkably vivid and fresh about Augustine's writing, and indeed they are mainly reflections and comments upon his own life and experiences, but they are not, it seems to me, reflections on Augustine's direct experiences of God. Further, whilst the *Confessions* show a remarkable level of self analysis, or introspection, they are mainly Augustine speaking to God, or reports of Augustine speaking to God rather than reports of God speaking to Augustine. Critically perhaps there is no element of union, and no intimation that Augustine's personality is somehow lost, wrapped up totally in the Divine, and so whilst one can recognises a spiritual depth I do not think it appropriate to consider Augustine as a mystic or as a mystic theologian.

By contrast S. Francis is often described as a mystic. This claim rests centrally on Francis having received the stigmata. In the late summer of 1224 Francis had withdrawn for refreshment and prayer, and during a period of intense prayer at La Verna marks of the crucifixion appeared on his hands and his feet and his right side became as though it had been pierced with a lance. The meaning of these marks is generally understood as a sign of a profound identification of Francis with Christ; Francis shared in Christ's death in a spectacularly intimate way, and was assured by Christ of great intimacy and union.

It is said that Francis made every effort to hide the stigmata and only a few people were initially privileged to see them, but over time more people did see them, and later witnesses gave evidence and testimony of them under oath (c.f. Robson p264). At his death Francis is said to have had himself placed naked on the earth. In his final hour he gave away even his clothes and prepared to return to the dust from whence he had come. At this time many would presumably have seen the stigmata. Gregory IX subsequently preached about Francis' stigmata and published documents about them, and clearly recognised them as a mark of Francis' closeness or mystic union with his divine Master.

Francis' adoration of and intimacy with the created order was not the intimacy of a naturalist or biologist, but was the intimacy of a mystic who saw the divine hand in all that He had made. Francis saw no division between the natural and the spiritual and saw that everything was created by God. As such, both natural or material objects as well as the supernatural were revered by Francis as bearers of God's truth; and through all things he was able to enjoy an intimate communion with God.

Something of this communion with creation is to be found in Francis' *Canticle of Brother Sun*, which I considered above, but which in the context shows a remarkable union between Francis and the created order and, by extension, with God. Quoting Celano's *vita prima*, Robson says "he discerned the hidden things of nature with his sensitive heart, as one who had already escaped into the freedom of the glory of the sons of God" (Robson p244). Francis was then almost certainly a mystic, but to what extent Anthony would have been aware of this, it is hard to say. I have suggested that he had probably read Francis' Canticle and he may well have heard of Francis' stigmata, but whether that constituted anything of a Franciscan 'mystical tradition' of which S. Anthony could have been a part seems doubtful.

Finally I want to reconsider the influence of Hugh of S. Victor on S. Anthony. Hugh's influence on Anthony has already been mentioned in the context of Biblical study and a marked Christocentric theological outlook, and the claim has been made that Anthony would have been aware of Hugh and his school in Paris via links with the Coimbra Augustinians. A further dimension to this link is that Hugh was a noted mystic.

Hugh was primarily a lecturer of philosophy and theology, and his most significant written works concern these disciplines. However for Hugh these academic disciplines were not ends in themselves but were a means, a path to closer union with God. Furthermore, intense thought and the religious life were not to be isolated from each other, but were a part of a unified whole. Thought, meditation and contemplation respectively allow us to discover God in the material world, God within ourselves and God as supernatural and divinely 'other'. These three modes of seeking God were the 'three eyes' of the rational soul. Hugh's mystical writings are but a small part of his corpus, but *de arca noe morali et mystica, de vanitate mundi, de arrha animae* and *de contemplatione et eius speciebus* are significant medieval mystical texts, part or all of which, it is not unreasonable to suppose, Anthony may have read. So let us turn to the key question: was Anthony himself a mystic?

Anthony is most frequently portrayed in art holding the child Jesus. This derives from an event which most accounts of his life place in Camposampiero (near Padua) while Anthony was enjoying the hospitality of Count Tiso. Anthony having retired to bed, the count noticed a bright light from under Anthony's bedroom door and peeping through the keyhole, or through a crack in the door, he saw Anthony with the child Jesus. Anthony spoke to the infant and was permitted to embrace him, and was in turn blessed by him. Like most such events the count was sworn to secrecy until after Anthony's death, and whilst 'the cell of the vision' still exists today, we cannot after many years be sure of what really happened. To add further confusion, other accounts of Anthony's life record the same event, but locate it in France.

What we can be sure of, is that this miracle, or at any rate this enduring legend about S. Anthony shows or is meant to show a deep intimacy between Anthony and Jesus. In some artistic depictions it almost seems as if Anthony and Jesus are playing together. The iconography demonstrates not only an intimacy, but perhaps suggests that Anthony himself was as a little child, (Matt 18:3), not childish but unencumbered, honest, trusting and loving.

Jack Wintz has suggested that the meaning of the vision is a confirmation or an underlining of the fact that as Anthony was unquestionably intimate with holy scripture, the word of God, he was also intimate with the divine Word of God – the Son of the Father (c.f. Wintz p28-35). Wintz also suggests that there was a legend of the child Jesus appearing to Francis in a crib scene, upon the straw, and that the appearance of the child Jesus to Anthony was "a kind of 'copycat' story" (Wintz p30). Not 'copycat' in the sense of a crude hagiography, but in the sense that as Francis was intimate with the Lord, with the child Jesus in fact, so too was S. Anthony.

Additional evidence may be gained from the documented friendship of Anthony with Abbott Thomas Gallo of Vercelli, a master of the spiritual life, who was known for translating the work of Denis the Areopagite from the Greek, and writing a commentary. There is no record that Anthony ever attended any of the formal classes that Abbott Thomas gave, but there is strong suggestion that Anthony visited him several times and that they exchanged views on mystical theology (c.f. Huber p12).

The Abbott wrote of Anthony that "aided by divine grace he drew most abundantly from the mystical theology of the sacred scriptures" (From the *Legenda Benignitas* quoted in Huber), and the author of the Legenda Prima quotes the Abbott again as saying; "I was able to experience in that holy friar, Anthony, of the Order of Friars Minor whose friendship I had the pleasure of enjoying. He – thanks to the purity of his soul and the flame of divine love, which burned in his heart – was drawn with great ardour of mind and fervour of spirit towards mystical theology and acquired it on so large a scale that one would be tempted to say of him what was written of S. John the Baptist that he was a '*lucerna, ardens et lucens*' because burning interiorly, due to his great love, he could not but shine exteriorly" (Huber p82).

Finally evidence for Anthony being a mystic is perhaps offered by the suggestion that Anthony wrote a work on mysticism: *expositio mystica in sacram scripturam.* Rohr and Huber both suggest that this is not a genuine work of S. Anthony, but that the text is Anthony's. That is to say that this supposed work is a later compilation of Anthony's writings on mystical themes in holy scripture, and indeed Rohr shows convincingly that passages from *expositio mystica* may be found in the sermons. Rohr suggests that a later compiler has "gathered the saint's explanations of various scriptural passages from the sermons and arranged them in the order of the books of the bible" (Rohr 90).

If we examine the three passages that Rohr quotes, which appear both in the *expositio mystica* and the Sermons and which could, Rohr says, "be multiplied many times" (Rohr p92) what do we find? In the first extract, Anthony is discussing God's mercy, judgement and power and quotes Job to the effect that "He commandeth the sun and it riseth not" (Job 9:7). He says that "the sun stands for the illumination of grace, which rises when it is infused into the mind, and rises not when it is not granted" (Spilsbury I p378).

In the second extract Anthony is discussing Christ's care for us and he quotes Jeremiah saying "I see a branch of the watchful tree" (Jer 1.11). Anthony says the watchful tree, "the rod, strong and green, and a symbol of ruling power, stands for Jesus Christ" (Spilsbury I p195). Anthony develops the rod image in an unusual way, noting that as thieves steal from the houses of those who sleep using a rod with a hook attached to it (!) so Christ hooks souls from the devil, using the rod of his humanity and the hook of his holy cross (c.f. Spilsbury I p196).

In the final passage that Huber shows is both in *expositio mystica* and Anthony's sermons, Anthony offers a moral interpretation of the story of David's defeat of the Philistines. The Philistines are likened to those who live lives according to bodily senses and fall into sin. David's defeat of these is likened to the defeat of bodily desires by the penitent who mortifies his flesh (c.f.Spilsbury III p60).

I would suggest that what links all of these passages is not a concern with mystical theology, nor a concern for the meaningful exposition of mystical experience, but simply an interpretation of scripture. The enthusiast who compiled this selection of Anthony's works may have considered Anthony's explanations as revealing something hidden in scripture, and in that limited sense, mystical; but in the sense that I have outlined there is nothing mystical about these passages at all. I would go further and say that Anthony's oeuvre as a whole has very little if anything to say about mystical theology and the interpretation of mystic experience.

As I shall say again later, I think one of the key aspects of S. Anthony and his life is balance, and whilst Anthony may well, and in my opinion certainly did have a very lively prayer life and was particularly attuned to the divine, he was also a practical man; involved in preaching, teaching, travelling and governing a rapidly developing religious order. His writings, which are his sermons, are practical guides for his brother friars and there is no textual evidence and indeed there would have been no reason for him to dwell on abstract notions of mystical theology.

Indeed, whilst I do not profess to be any expert on these matters, I cannot help but feel that Huber rather overstates the case when he suggests that Anthony prepared the way for S. Bonaventure, S. Thomas and S. Theresa and when he cites Father Heerinckx OFM approvingly to the effect that Anthony may even be seen as the mystical forerunner of S. John of the Cross (Huber p81). Anthony is considered milder and more accessible than his austere Carmelite successor, he says, and three centuries before John of the Cross, Anthony "teaches the classical doctrines of the passive, sensitive and intellectual activities of the soul along with the *via purgativa* and the *noce obscura*" (ibid).

It may well be that Anthony's mysticism, or consideration of "matters of the highest speculative nature" (Huber p81) avoids some of the excesses and fallacies of other writers, being firmly rooted in S. Augustine, S. Gregory the Great and Hugh of S. Victor, but to claim that Anthony paved the way for Bonaventure *et al.* in the field of mystical theology is a claim that, to my mind, requires considerably more textual evidence than is available.

By contrast, Anton Rotzetter observes that for much of his early life Anthony exercised his own will, joining the Augustinians, petitioning to be transferred to Coimbra, leaving the Augustinians, joining the Franciscans, petitioning to be sent to Morocco etc. But in his sickness in Morocco and his subsequent shipwreck in Sicily, Anthony had to learn that he was unable to make all his own decisions and that he "was now at the mercy and hands of God, and willing to do only what he was called to do" (Rotzetter p11). Anthony must have reflected at length and prayed about these events and Rotzetter suggests this is the key to Anthony's understanding of the passivity of the soul, the understanding that true freedom is placing oneself unconditionally into the hands of God.

I am inclined to agree more with this analysis, but this is an analysis of Anthony's life, albeit his spiritual life. It tells us how Anthony may have thought, and how he developed. It tells us of the man and not of his teaching or his theology, although of course, these events give us valuable background and help us to better understand S. Anthony's text.

So to return to the two questions I posed at the beginning of this section: was S. Anthony a mystic, and may we additionally regard Anthony as a mystic theologian? I think the answer to the first question is probably yes. I think Anthony had a particular awareness of God's presence and I think the biographical details concerning his prayer life and the many miracles he performed do support the contention that Anthony was something of a mystic. However I do not think there is any convincing evidence to suggest that Anthony analysed, classified or interpreted in writing any of the mystic experiences he (or others) may have had, and so in that sense I do not think Anthony can be said to be a mystic theologian. (The precise content of any conversations that Anthony may have had with Abbott Thomas can really be no more than speculation.) The mystic theologian is not a theologian who is also a mystic, the mystic theologian is a theologian who concerns himself in his studies, or in an academic way with mystical theology, and I think there is little or no evidence that S. Anthony did this.

Section Three

In Search of the Evangelical Doctor

3.1   The Legacy of S. Anthony

S. Anthony died on 13 June 1231 and many miracles surrounded his funeral and burial. The Assidua tells us, "That same day there were carried to the tomb of the saint very many people suffering from various illness, and immediately they were cured and restored to their original health through the merits of blessed Anthony" (Gamboso p54). There was much devotion and religious fervour and within a month of his death, delegates were sent from Padua to the Apostolic Sea petitioning for the canonisation of Anthony.

As is customary Pope Gregory IX in consultation with his cardinals examined the documents surrounding Anthony's cause and noted the miracles worked at his intercession. In remarkably quick time, indeed within a year, the evidence had been duly considered and at the cathedral at Spoleto, Anthony was solemnly declared a saint by Gregory IX, at Pentecost, 30 May 1232. It is said that so joyful was the celebration that Gregory IX was overcome by emotion and after the hymn, he intoned the antiphon (for the Magnificat) *O Doctor Optime*, although Anthony was not formally declared a doctor at the time. Clasen suggests that Pope Gregory only wished to indicate the reverence that should be accorded to Anthony "as a wonderful preacher, teacher and writer" (Clasen p110).

In the bull of canonisation, Gregory refers to Anthony's many merits, his confounding of heresy and his encouragement of true catholic belief. He refers to his virtuous character, his miraculous acts and his holiness. He describes him as a lamp to be put upon a stand and as a great confessor and he further commendeds Anthony's tomb to the whole church as one to be fittingly honoured and visited. Indeed an indulgence was granted to anyone making a reverent visit to the tomb on S. Anthony's feast (13 June) or during the octave.

In the years following Anthony's death, the nature of theology changed: prayerful meditation, a consideration of etymologies and a following of concordances gave way to a more 'modern' approach as advocated by the new universities of Oxford and Paris which focussed on logical argument and deduction. Systemisation and systematic theology, as supremely exemplified by the Summae of S. Thomas Aquinas, were the order of the day, and Anthony's work fell into neglect. As Spilsbury puts it in his article in the *Messenger of St Anthony* "He was the final flowering of an earlier age, to be revered but not necessarily imitated" (Jan 2006 p13).

Additionally, within his own order (in the thirteenth century at least) Anthony was to be somewhat eclipsed. Bonaventure was born near Orvieto in 1221 and joined the Franciscans in 1243. He was sent to Paris to study and was influenced by the school of Hugh of S. Victor, and by the new scholastic school of theology which derived ultimately from the rediscovery of Aristotle, and was a development of his logical and systematic approach. Bonaventure gained his teaching licence around 1248 and for a time at least, was a contemporary of Aquinas at the new University of Paris.

In 1257 Bonaventure was elected eighth minister general of the Franciscan Order, and having been influential in the election of Gregory X as Pope, he was duly made Cardinal Archbishop of Albano in 1273. Bonaventure died during the Council of Lyons in 1274. He was canonised as a saint in 1482 and declared a Doctor of the Church, the 'Seraphic Doctor', in 1588.

As minister general of the friars minor, Bonaventure is frequently considered as the 'second founder of the order'. Despite the bull *Quo Elongati* (1230) mentioned above, disagreements about the interpretation of Francis' rule rumbled on. As the friars had an increasing presence in the new universities, how was Franciscan poverty to be understood, and how was an administrative system to be developed to accommodate the ever increasing number of friars and friaries? In short there seemed to be a general decline in apostolic zeal: had the new order lost its way?

Bonaventure adopted a balanced approach, keeping close to the original spirit of S. Francis, but he rejected the extremes of those (who came to be known as the 'spirituals') who believed that poverty was the single most important feature of the order. He supported the presence of the friars at the universities, and he supported learning both as a means to a deeper spirituality, and as a tool for preaching and teaching the people. Crucially in his *Disputed Questions on Evangelical Perfection*, he contextualises poverty. He says poverty is not an end in itself but is a way, a means to humility and charity. Further, poverty is not to be understood as poverty at any given instant, but is poverty of a whole Christian life. It is a recognition that we have nothing of ourselves and are wholly dependent on God. As S. Anthony himself expressed it "Do you want to keep what you have received? Then attribute it to God not yourself. If you give yourself credit for what is not yours, you are guilty of theft" (Spilsbury II p391).

For Bonaventure charity is the *principium fundamentale*, and is to be served by poverty, but poverty itself is not an end. Christ was poor on account of his charity and in imitating Christ the brothers are to imitate his charity first and foremost, with poverty as a powerful means to that end.

Bonaventure also maintained a unity within the order which by this time had thousands of brothers in thirty-six provinces. He wrote many letters and many Franciscan historians regard his generalate as "a blessing in which his moderation saved the order from chaos" (Cullen p13). In the light of Bonaventure's theological ability and his general influence on the Franciscan order, it is perhaps no surprise that S. Anthony was at least side-lined if not neglected.

Some three hundred years later, the liturgical reforms of Pope S. Pius V (the breviary in 1568 and the missal in 1570) abolished the feast of S. Anthony along with many others, and although it was subsequently restored by Sixtus V in 1585, Anthony was given the status of a simple confessor. Only in Franciscan circles and in Franciscan liturgies was Anthony celebrated with any solemnity.

In the light of this decline it may seem something of a surprise that on 16 January 1946, over seven hundred years after his canonisation, S. Anthony was declared a Doctor of the Universal Church and given the title of *Doctor Evangelicus.* How then did this come about?

The formalities are to be found in the encyclical *Exulta Lusitania felix* in which Pope Pius XII declares Anthony to be "a man not unlike a brilliant star........by the radiant splendour of heavenly doctrine he has illumined the whole world." And again later he says, "Anthony is revealed as most skilled in sacred scripture, as a remarkable theologian of the teachings of our faith and as an exceptional teacher and master in ascetical and mystical subjects" *(Exulta).* Pius notes the intoning of the antiphon *O Doctor Optime* by his predecessor and says he "willingly and gladly accedes to the petitions of all the Franciscans and other petitioners.....to declare S. Anthony of Padua, Confessor, a Doctor of the universal Church" (ibid).

There is a real sense of joy in the document, a sense of completing what was perhaps in some way overdue and giving Anthony recognition on account of his theological mastery. It is perhaps fitting that Anthony was finally placed alongside his own heroes, Augustine and Bernard, Gregory the Great and Isidore, not to mention his successor S. Bonaventure, and it is also eminently fitting that the declaration was made on the feast of the Franciscan Protomartyrs, those five who first roused Anthony to leave the confines of his priory and to become a peripatetic preacher and teacher of the Gospel.

This declaration is however more fully understood if it is seen in its appropriate historical context. At the beginning of the twentieth century the world was changing very fast. Huge advances in science and technology were being made and in artistic and philosophical circles modernism was sweeping Europe. The conservative Pope S. Pius X (1903 – 1914) saw his role as protecting the church and the faithful against these advances, and his 1907 encyclical *Pascendi et Lamentabili* condemned modernism, defined as the synthesis of all heresies. An anti-modernism oath was enjoined on the clergy, and Catholic scholars were bound to conform to central curial authority.

Meanwhile, protestant biblical scholars especially those in Germany were employing all the latest literary methods in the analysis of biblical texts. They analysed the texts with the latest scientific, linguistic and exegetical apparatus, which inevitably led them to question some if not many of the received, and from the then catholic point of view, inerrant, understandings of the text. The church entrenched itself and the encyclical *Spiritus Paraclitus* promulgated by Pope Benedict XV in 1920 strongly defended the historicity of the Bible.

By the middle of the twentieth century the Catholic Church realised it had lost the initiative as far as biblical science was concerned, and a renaissance in biblical studies began. The pontificate of Pius XII (1939-1958) saw something of a *volte-face* as far as biblical studies were concerned, and the ground-breaking encyclical *Divino Afflante Spiritu* of 1943 announced that the time of fear of modernism was over and that catholic biblical scholars should use all modern tools available to further critical understanding of the Bible. In particular scholars were encouraged to reconsider the biblical texts in their original languages and to improve and update translations where appropriate. A free and open discussion concerning the dating and authorship of the biblical texts was also encouraged.

All this work needed a patron, a renowned biblical exegete and scholar, a Catholic hero to champion the cause, to encourage and indeed by his intercession, guide this work. In this light the declaration of Anthony as the Evangelical Doctor was both timely and appropriate. Alongside the unprecedented number of Cardinals Pius XII created in two consistories and the large number (thirty-three) of saints he canonised his declaration of Anthony as a Doctor is in keeping with his generally busy and outward looking papacy.

The successor of Pope Pius XII was Pope John XXIII (1958-1963) who is best remembered perhaps for convoking the Second Vatican Council. This council was intended to bring about a regeneration of the Church, to review and revise doctrine, liturgy, discipline (canon law), organisation and so on. Many scholars believe that the ramifications of this council are still to be fully worked through and implemented and there is ongoing discussion about how radical the changes implemented by the council really were, but the relevance for us is the claim made by Fr Claude M Jarmak OFM that "many of the questions touched upon in the Second Vatican Council are discussed in Anthony's *Opus*" (Jarmak p219). This does not amount to a claim that Anthony's theology directly influenced the deliberations of the council, or that among the many theological influences Anthony was in any way unique, but it is the observation that many of the conciliar themes were prefigured in Anthony's writings and that striking parallels may be found.

Firstly, in the Dogmatic Constitution on Divine Revelation, *Dei Verbum* there is a renewed emphasis on the place of holy scripture in the liturgical celebrations of the church. The Council taught that the Mass was not simply an occasion to receive the sacrament of the Eucharist, but that it was an occasion to hear and be nourished by the Word of God in holy scripture. The church "never ceases, particularly in the sacred liturgy, to partake of the bread of life and to offer it to the faithful from the one table of the Word of God and the Body of Christ" (DV 21, Flannery p762).

Over seven hundred years previously, S. Anthony wrote, "Thy children as olive shoots round about thy table.....Note that the table is threefold and each has its proper refreshment. The first is of teaching....the second is of penitence.....the third is that of the Eucharist" (Spilsbury IV p55, 59).

Modes of expression and details of number may vary, but the underlying point is the same: God feeds us not only through the sacrament of the Eucharist, but through sacred scripture, and the lectern and the altar are corresponding pieces of liturgical furniture. In Anthony's terminology the correspondence is expressed in that they are both tables, on which 'food' albeit of different kinds is laid out.

Secondly, in the Dogmatic Constitution on the Church, *Lumen Gentium*, the Fathers, reflecting on Paul's teaching that "All of us, though there are so many of us, make up one body in Christ" (Rom 12:5), teach that within the church there is a diversity of offices and functions. The fathers also teach that the church is hierarchically arranged, but over and over they emphasise that the call to holiness is universal. Sanctity of life is not just for priests and bishops but "All Christians in any state or walk of life are called to the fullness of Christian life and to the perfection of love, and by this holiness a more human manner of life is fostered also in earthly society" (LG 40, Flannery p397). All are called to imitate the Lord and by grace to conform themselves to his image.

Anthony wrote that "The sons of Christ should walk in newness of spirit and by confession renew their spirit day by day...thus says the Lord to the men of Judah and Jerusalem" (Spilsbury IV p59). The address to the men of Judah and Jerusalem is a quotation from the prophet Jeremiah (4:3) which signifies an address to both clergy (Jerusalem) and laity (Judah). All Christian people are called to be "united with Christ in the church and marked with the Holy Spirit "who is the guarantee of our inheritance" (Eph 1:14)" (LG 48, Flannery p408).

To consider one final example, the council's recognition of the special place of the poor in the church is a teaching that was dear to Anthony too. In the Pastoral Constitution on the Church in the Modern World, *Gaudium et Spes*, the fathers teach that "while there are rightful differences between people, their equal dignity as persons demands that we strive for fairer and more humane conditions. Excessive economic and social disparity between individuals and peoples of the one human race is a source of scandal, and militates against social justice, equity, human dignity, as well as social and international peace" (GS29, Flannery p930).

These are strong words indeed, but as Jarmak remarks, for Anthony too "religion was not only vertical, that is directed towards God in heaven but also horizontal, that is, extending itself outward to other people, not only in spiritual, but also in material things (Jarmak p225). Perhaps taking his cue from Francis, who as we noted was struck that the wealth of the rich is all too often at the expense of the poor Anthony condemns "the rich and powerful of this world [who] look down upon the poor as their inferiors, while they themselves are subjects of the devil. They take from them the poor and bloodstained livelihood with which, somehow, they cover themselves" (Spilsbury II p249). Anthony also quotes the prophet Jeremiah "the very skirts of your robe are stained with the blood of the poor (Jer 2:34)" (ibid).

Anthony not only preached about the plight of the poor, but famously acted to have the law amended. As commerce grew and the use of money replaced bartering and trading goods for goods, banks developed and lending became established. Inevitably there were those who could not repay their debts, and with accumulating interest payments, the gap between rich and poor grew. At the time people who were unable to pay their debts could be imprisoned.

On 15 March 1231 the legal authorities in Padua enacted a new law "At the request of the venerable and holy brother Anthony, confessor of the Order of Friars Minor, no one, whether a debtor or a guarantor, is to be deprived of his personal freedom in the future if he is unable to pay. In such a case he may be deprived of his property, but not of his personal freedom" (Jarmak p225). This clearly demonstrates not only Anthony's awareness and concern for the plight of the poor, but also shows a willingness and an ability to engage with secular officials to effect social change, to the advantage of the poor. Anthony was no less scandalised by economic and social disparity, than were the authors of *Gaudium et Spes*.

Perhaps S. Anthony's most lasting legacy is prayer. I do

not mean theory or teaching about prayer, but the many prayers he himself wrote (some of which we have already seen in his sermons) and the many traditions of praying to S. Anthony which have become a real part of daily catholic life. How many catholic churches have a statue of S. Anthony and how many catholics invoke Anthony's assistance when they have lost their car keys, glasses or whatever? This is not blasphemy but is a recognition of Anthony's holiness and in our attempts to become more like Anthony we ourselves are on the road to becoming more like Christ himself. As Pope Pius XI said in his centenary letter, *Antoniana Solemnia* of September 1931, *per Antonium ad Jesum!*

Perhaps mindful of the words of S. Francis that his (Anthony's) teaching should not extinguish the spirit of prayer, the Sermons contain some sixty prayers, approximately one at the end of each sermon. These prayers have a remarkable freshness and vibrancy to them. They are written simply but are well-formed, and as Spilsbury says "Anthony's Latin is simple and elegant" (Spilsbury I px). In general the prayers are fairly brief, but on occasion as if Anthony wants to develop a particular theme (e.g. light) they become quite lengthy. For Quinquagesima he writes:

"Let us pray then dear brethren and ask straightway for devotion of mind,

So that our Lord Jesus Christ who gave light to the man born blind,

To Tobias and to the Angel of Laodicea may be pleased to illuminate the eyes of our souls with the faith of his incarnation and the ointment of his passion.

Thus may we be able to see the Son of God himself, the Light of Light,

In the splendour of the saints and the brightness of the Angels.

May he grant this, who lives and reigns with the Father and the Holy Spirit, for ever and ever, Amen"

(Spilsbury I p67).

In the modern Roman Breviary (The Divine Office) almost all the collects are addressed to God the Father usually beginning; 'Lord God...', 'Almighty God...', 'Holy Father and Lord...' etc. On the feast of *Corpus Christi* the prayer is addressed to the God the Son: 'Lord Jesus Christ...' but this is exceptional. By comparison and quite significantly almost all of Anthony's prayers are addressed to God the Son, usually beginning 'Let us pray that the Lord Jesus Christ....'or 'We pray you then Lord Jesus...' Similarly the ending (doxology) tends to be along the lines; 'To him be honour and glory for ever and ever, Amen'.

There are exceptions of course and on the feast of Pentecost Anthony's prayer is addressed to the Holy Spirit. He prays: "Let us speak, then, as the Holy Spirit gives us to speak, asking him humbly and devoutly..." (ibid p 423). Similarly the Sermons for the Marian feasts end with prayers addressed to Mary, and as we have already seen Anthony tends to open these prayers 'We ask you Our Lady...', and end them with an invocation to God the Son. For example; 'May he grant this, who today deigned to be born of you' (Spilsbury III p413) or 'May he grant this, whom you today offered in the temple' (ibid p427).

It is also worth noting what Anthony prays for. On the one hand grace and faith are very regularly asked for and on the other hand a sense of contrition and forgiveness. Also wisdom, humility, patience, obedience, joy and peace are sought. Anthony's prayers are for divine grace and for virtue, often ending with the plea that by these he and all Christians may come to share the joys of heaven, in the company of the saints and the presence of the Father.

Since Anthony's death many special prayers and devotions to S. Anthony have been devised. There are the nine and the thirteen Tuesdays, the Chaplet of S. Anthony, the litany of S. Anthony, the blessing of S. Anthony's lilies and S. Anthony's brief to safeguard letters in the mail, to mention a few. Most common of course are the invocations to S. Anthony to help find lost objects. I do not wish to examine the origin and history of all these devotions here, but as I said above, I do not see them as misplaced for they foster a sense of ceaseless prayer. Prayer should not be something done in time set apart (although it may be) but is rather an integral part of a Christian day.

It was said of S. Francis by his biographer Thomas of Celano that he did not pray, but that his whole life, his whole being had become prayer. For Anthony too, as we have seen, prayer was an integral part of all that he did; his work of teaching and preaching was wrapped up in prayer, and prayer animated all that he did. To the extent that Anthony's devotions are regular and infuse our daily lives they help us to pray unceasingly and have the potential to animate and infuse all that we do too.

For me this is the central and most fundamental teaching of S. Anthony and deserves to be his principal legacy. The work of prayer, listening to God and sharing our lives with God is not simply the task of priests, monks and nuns, it is not a fundamentally 'other' activity that has to take place at specially allotted times and in particular places (although it can be these). Prayer is an ongoing orientation of the person towards God, it is a product of everything else that we do and are, and also in a reciprocal manner is the source, and provides the means for all that we undertake and all that we have to do.

Religious have traditionally been considered as active or contemplative, working in the world or withdrawing from the world, a distinction that is said to derive from the story of Mary and Martha in Luke 10. It seems to me that Anthony's life and his teaching cuts straight through this: almost without exception Christians are called to be active *and* contemplative. They are to engage in ministry, family life, a job of work and so on and they are to pray. Work leads to prayer, to a longing for God, to a yearning for refreshment and sustenance. Prayer leads to refreshment, regeneration and inspiration for what is to come.

Anthony, as I have suggested, was a scholar, an academic and a teacher – this was his 'work', but it was completely integrated with a profound life of prayer, and a holiness of life. Anthony's own life suggests to me that Francis' injunction to teach, but not so as to extinguish a commitment to prayer was, at least for Anthony, a vacuous command. For Anthony love of God found in prayer led to study, and study of holy scripture and of God, led to prayer.

This fundamental lesson was recognised by Bonaventure who stabilised the early Order when it threatened to tear itself apart. More importantly however it is a lesson in every age, and in particular it is a lesson for us, that prayer and work go hand in hand and if we have the inclination or the ability this translates to prayer and study. S. Anthony taught by words and by his writing but above all, like Francis, he taught by his example. His life, though short, was a life immersed in work and fervent prayer and as such is a template and an example for us all.

3.2   Conclusion

On 16 January 1996, the fiftieth anniversary of the proclamation of S. Anthony as Doctor of the Church, the late Pope John Paul II wrote an open letter to the Franciscan Minister General, the Most Reverend Bonaventure Midili, by way of celebration of the occasion. The letter itself, written in Italian, is not long, merely five sections, but I want to use it as a focus and as an aid to bring my own thoughts to a conclusion.

John Paul II begins by reaffirming S. Anthony to be a master of theology and of the spiritual life, having a profound understanding of scripture and the gift of being able to preach Christ to the world. He emphasises that for Anthony study was born from a love of Christ, and that Anthony was both a man of wisdom and a man of charity (*"uomo evangelico rivestito di sapienza e di carità"*).

In the second and longest of the five sections Pope John Paul II expands his theme, and declares that Anthony's theological mastery was derived from his cultural background, his biblical study and formation, and his immersion in the liturgy of the church. Furthermore he adds that this mastery was fed by holiness (*"alimentata da intensa pietà"*) which derived from prayer and contemplation of the mysteries of Christ. He repeats this towards the end of the letter, asserting that S. Anthony, with the eyes of faith, beheld the true splendour of the triune God through prayer and contemplation, and further from the riches of his mind and in communion with the church he transmitted this to others.

John Paul goes on to note the context in which all this happened, an age when cultural and ethical innovations were being made independently of the church. An age when heresy of one kind or another was widespread and an age when civil institutions were beginning to grow, and beginning to exercise authority and power. He emphasises that Anthony's teaching had a strong ecclesial dimension and that his powerful moral teaching (*esortazione morale*) was that the good life had to be a life in the church and with the church.

John Paul concludes this section with a reference to poverty which he describes as 'golden poverty' *(aurea paupertas)*. He emphasises that poverty, beloved of the Franciscan Order is not only a separation from the concerns of the world, but is a fundamental orientation towards the things of heaven. Reminiscent of Bonaventure the Pope reminds us that poverty is not an end in itself but is a means or a way towards the things of heaven (*cose celesti*).

In a short third section Anthony's ecclesial stance is further endorsed and John Paul writes that only within the church is the fullness of truth to be found. The church following Christ who is the truth (Jn 14:6) and inspired by the action of the Holy Spirit, is the good and fertile field (*terra bona e feconda*) from which all truth springs. In view of this the church is able to preserve us from all dangers and through its preaching of the word of God, is able to give us inner peace.

A fourth section emphasises the manner and style of Anthony's preaching rather than its content. John Paul writes of Anthony's assiduous evangelisation and indefatigable preaching. We are reminded that the strength for this comes from the sacraments, primarily from penance and the Eucharist, but here we get a real sense of the urgency and the purpose to be found in Anthony's work. Anthony was not a half-hearted preacher but a man of energy and charisma who brought not only learning and holiness to his task but great strength of purpose.

It is this sense of purpose, this vitality that John Paul urges on the Franciscan family. He urges and encourages them to find anew the prayerful theology and the evangelical praxis of the saint. He suggests academic reflection, accompanied by prayer and grounded in the church, is what is required in the contemporary world, and he urges the '*confratelli*' of the evangelical doctor to continue their work of preaching and teaching with vigour (*con intensificata vigore*) and ecclesial fidelity.

John Paul concludes his message with an apostolic blessing on all Franciscans, and generously extends it to all who are devotees of the saint (*a tutti i devoti del Santo*).

I think two key points which summarise the life and work of S. Anthony emerge from a consideration of this document. Firstly that S. Anthony was undoubtedly a scholar, a biblical theologian of great ability and an extraordinary preacher and teacher. I think there is something of a recognition that a prayerful and meditative approach to biblical theology which became unfashionable shortly after Anthony's death has a place in modern theological study and that Anthony's theology had a clarity and an insight worthy of special note.

Secondly I feel that John Paul hints at but does not fully develop the thought that Anthony most successfully integrated his life of study with a life of prayer. I think this is most undoubtedly the case, but I think more generally Anthony's greatness lies in the fact that the many facets of his life were so harmoniously integrated. In our modern life we 'pigeon-hole' people as doctors or teachers, lawyers or theologians, men of thought or men of action etc. Anthony was all of these things. He thought and he did. He worked and he prayed. He lived in community and he found time to spend apart with God.

In a wider sense, he lived at a time when inward-looking, Augustinian-Benedictine monastic spirituality was beginning to give way to an outward-looking mendicant spirituality. There was a change in emphasis from an interior devotion to an external form of devotion, centred on preaching and care for the poor. I think these changes in emphasis reflect to some extent historical changes in the world, and I think that as thesis and antithesis there will always be a dynamic between these approaches to the religious life. In Anthony however we see both. We see a man whose life was founded on a relationship of prayer with God and who was also a man fully engaged with the world. We see a man who transcended the either-or dichotomy to embrace the both-and position. And as such we see a man who was supremely at peace with himself, not stressed or troubled but balanced and happy.

Of course, Anthony was not at peace with himself through his own psychological effort, as in the sense of a modern self help guide, but his interior peace was a consequence of his deep, and lively relationship with God. Anthony recognised that God was the source and the motivation of his whole life and he was able not only to assent to this intellectually, but to live this belief. Anthony was a scholar, but he was a holy man too. In him study and virtue were combined, considerable stature and perfect humility, work and prayer – a man more than worthy to be a doctor of the universal church.

In this work I have considered Anthony primarily as a mediaeval academic; I have considered those who influenced him, what he wrote and those whom he influenced. I have deliberately set myself to avoid the oft-repeated biographical details of his life, especially the many accounts of the miracles he wrought. To conclude I am going to break my own rules, so to speak, and recount the miracle of S. Anthony that is my favourite.

It is said that Anthony was entertained by a well-wisher one Friday evening and the well-wisher gave Anthony poussin to eat. Not wishing to offend his host Anthony ate the poussin although it was neither vegetarian nor fish. Self righteous onlookers were apparently shocked that this holy man would eat meat on a Friday, against the teaching of the church, and called the local bishop to come and rule on the matter. The bishop duly arrived and Anthony's plate was examined, but it was found that the remains of the poussin had miraculously transformed into the perfect skeleton of a fish!

It would be perverse to suppose that Anthony had performed this miracle to save himself from any trouble, and surely we must conclude that he did it in order to preserve his host from any trouble or embarrassment. Anthony as ever, was courteous and kind, thinking of others before himself, in the face of those who without any regard for charity were bound to the letter of the law.

For me I think it also shows that S. Anthony of Padua, biblical scholar, preacher extraordinaire, man of prayer and mystic, wonder-worker and doctor of the universal church had something of a sense of humour too.

Anthony of Padua – Pray for us

Bibliography

BROWN P. (1967) *Augustine of Hippo: A Biography* (Faber, London)

BROWN R. (ed.) *et al* (1989) *The New Jerome Biblical Commentary* (Chapman).

CLASEN S. (1973) *St Anthony Doctor of the Church* (Franciscan Herald Press, Chicago)

COOPER S.A. (2002) *Augustine for Armchair Theologians* (Westminster John Knox Press)

CULLEN C. M. (2006) *Bonaventure* (OUP)

FARMER D. H. (ed.) (1996) *Butler's Lives of the Saints. New Full Edition*. 12 vols.
(Burns & Oates)

FLANNERY A. (ed.) (1996) *Vatican Council II Volume I* (Costello Publishing Company, New York)

GAMBOSO V. (ed.) (1984) *Life of St Anthony "Assidua"* (Edizioni Messaggero Padova) (Reprinted 2006)

HARDICK L. (1989) *He came to you so that you might come to Him*
(Franciscan Herald Press, Chicago)

HUBER R. M. (1948) *St Anthony of Padua, Doctor of the Church Universal*
(Bruce Publishing Milwaukee)

KARRER O. (ed.) (1947) The *Little Flowers, Legends and Lauds*
(Sheed and Ward, London, trans. N. Wydenbruck)

JARMAK C. M. (1999) *If you seek miracles - Reflections of Saint Anthony of Padua*
(Edizioni Messaggero Padova)

LING S. W. (1995) *St Anthony of Padua, Friend of all the World*
(St Paul's UK)

McGINN B. (1991) *The Foundations of Mysticism, vol I of The Presence of God, A History of Western Christian Mysticism*
(New York Crossroad)

MERTON T. (1973) *Contemplation in a World of Action*
(Garden City, N.Y. Doubleday Image Books)

NUGENT M. P. (1996) *Praying with Saint Anthony of Padua*
(St Mary's Press Winona MN USA)

POLONIATO L. (1988) *Seek First His Kingdom: An anthology of the Sermons of the Saint*
(Editrice Grafiche Messaggero di S Antonio)

PORTALIÉ E. (1960) A *Guide to the Thought of Saint Augustine*
(Burns and Oates, London)

ROBSON M. (1997) *St Francis of Assisi*
(Geoffrey Chapman, London)

ROHR L. F. (1948) *The Use of Sacred Scripture in the Sermons of St Anthony of Padua*
(Catholic University of America Press, Washington)

ROTZETTER A. (2003) *St Anthony of Padua A Voice from Heaven*
(Catholic Book Publishing New York)

SOUTHERN R. W. (1990) *Saint Anselm: A Portrait in a Landscape* (CUP)

SPILSBURY P. (trans. & ed.) (2007) *Saint Anthony of Padua – Sermons for Sundays and Festivals Vol I* (Edizioni Messaggero di S. Antonio, Padova)

(2007) *Saint Anthony of Padua – Sermons for Sundays and Festivals Vol II* (Edizioni Messaggero di S. Antonio, Padova)

(2009) *Saint Anthony of Padua – Sermons for Sundays and Festivals Vol III* (Edizioni Messaggero di S. Antonio, Padova)

(2010) *Saint Anthony of Padua – Sermons for Sundays and Festivals Vol IV* (Edizioni Messaggero di S. Antonio, Padova)

VON BALTHASAR H. U. (1982) *The Von Balthazar Reader* (T & T Clarke, Edinburgh)

WEINANDY T. G. (2000) *Does God Suffer?* (T & T Clarke, Edinburgh)

WINTZ J. (ed.) (2005) St *Anthony of Padua: Saint of the People* (St Anthony Messenger Press USA)

WISEMAN, J. A. (2006) *Spirituality and Mysticism* (Orbis Books, New York)

WS - #0023 - 221220 - C0 - 216/138/11 - PB - 9781844269297 - Gloss Lamination